ANXIETY
AT 35,000 FEET

Other titles in the
Forensic Psychotherapy Monograph Series

Violence: A Public Health Menace and a Public Health Approach
   Edited by Sandra L. Bloom

Life within Hidden Walls: Psychotherapy in Prisons
   Edited by Jessica Williams Saunders

Forensic Psychotherapy and Psychopathology:
   Winnicottian Perspectives
   Edited by Brett Kahr

Dangerous Patients: A Psychodynamic Approach to Risk Assessment
   and Management
   Edited by Ronald Doctor

The Mind of the Paedophile: Psychoanalytic Perspectives
   Edited by Charles W. Socarides

ANXIETY
AT 35,000 FEET

An Introduction
to Clinical Aerospace Psychology

Robert Bor

with contributions by
Brett Kahr

Foreword by
Jane N. Zuckerman

Forensic Psychotherapy Monograph Series

Series Editor
Brett Kahr

Honorary Consultant
Estela Welldon

KARNAC

LONDON   NEW YORK

First published in 2004 by
H. Karnac (Books) Ltd.
6 Pembroke Buildings, London NW10 6RE

British Library Cataloguing in Publication Data

A C.I.P. for this book is available from the British Library

 ISBN: 1-85575-965-9

10 9 8 7 6 5 4 3 2 1

Edited, designed, and produced by Communication Crafts

Printed in Great Britain

www.karnacbooks.com

CONTENTS

SERIES FOREWORD   vii
ABOUT THE AUTHORS   xiii
FOREWORD by Jane N. Zuckerman   xv

1   Towards the development of
    clinical aerospace psychology   1

2   Understanding passenger behaviour   7

3   The mental health of pilots   39

4   The psychodynamics of travel phobia:
    a contribution to clinical aerospace psychology
            Brett Kahr   65

5   Clinical aerospace psychology in the future:
    a dialogue
            Robert Bor in conversation with Brett Kahr   71

REFERENCES   95
INDEX   103

SERIES FOREWORD

Brett Kahr

Centre for Child Mental Health, London
and
The Winnicott Clinic of Psychotherapy, London

Throughout most of human history, our ancestors have done rather poorly when dealing with acts of violence. To cite but one of many shocking examples, let us perhaps recall a case from 1801, of an English boy aged only 13, who was executed by hanging on the gallows at Tyburn. What was his crime? It seems that he had been condemned to die for having stolen a spoon (Westwick, 1940).

In most cases, our predecessors have either *ignored* murderousness and aggression, as in the case of Graeco–Roman infanticide, which occurred so regularly in the ancient world that it acquired an almost normative status (deMause, 1974; Kahr, 1994); or they have *punished* murderousness and destruction with retaliatory sadism, a form of unconscious identification with the aggressor. Any history of criminology will readily reveal the cruel punishments inflicted upon prisoners throughout the ages, ranging from beatings and stockades, to more severe forms of torture, culminating in eviscerations, beheadings, or lynchings.

Only during the last one hundred years have we begun to develop the capacity to respond more intelligently and more humanely to acts of dangerousness and destruction. Since the advent of psychoanalysis and psychoanalytic psychotherapy, we now have access to a much deeper understanding both of the aetiology of aggressive acts and of their treatment; and nowadays we need no longer ignore criminals or abuse them—instead, we can provide compassion and containment, as well as conduct research that can help to prevent future acts of violence.

The modern discipline of forensic psychotherapy, which can be defined, quite simply, as the use of psychoanalytically orientated "talking therapy" to treat violent, offender patients, stems directly from the work of Sigmund Freud. Almost one hundred years ago, at a meeting of the Vienna Psycho-Analytical Society, held on 6 February 1907, Sigmund Freud anticipated the clarion call of contemporary forensic psychotherapists when he bemoaned the often horrible treatment of mentally ill offenders, in a discussion on the psychology of vagrancy. According to Otto Rank, Freud's secretary at the time, the founder of psychoanalysis expressed his sorrow at the "nonsensical treatment of these people in prisons" (quoted in Nunberg & Federn, 1962, p. 108).

Many of the early psychoanalysts preoccupied themselves with forensic topics. Hanns Sachs, himself a trained lawyer, and Marie Bonaparte, the French princess who wrote about the cruelty of war, each spoke fiercely against capital punishment. Sachs, one of the first members of Freud's secret committee, regarded the death penalty for offenders as an example of group sadism (Moellenhoff, 1966). Bonaparte, who had studied various murderers throughout her career, had actually lobbied politicians in America to free the convicted killer Caryl Chessman, during his sentence on Death Row at the California State Prison in San Quentin, albeit unsuccessfully (Bertin, 1982).

Some years later, Melanie Klein concluded her first book, the landmark text *Die Psychoanalyse des Kindes* [*The Psycho-Analysis of Children*], with resounding passion about the problem of violence in our culture. Mrs Klein noted that acts of criminality invariably stem from disturbances in childhood, and that if young people could receive access to psychoanalytic treatment at any early age, then much cruelty could be prevented in later years. Klein expressed the hope that: "If every child who shows disturbances that are at all severe were to be analysed in good time, a great number of these people who later end up in prisons or lunatic asylums, or who go completely to pieces, would be saved from such a fate and be able to develop a normal life" (1932, p. 374).

Shortly after the publication of Klein's transformative book, Atwell Westwick, a Judge of the Superior Court of Santa Barbara, California, published a little-known though highly inspiring article, "Criminology and Psychoanalysis" (1940), in the *Psychoanalytic Quarterly*. Westwick may well be the first judge to commit himself in print to the value of psychoanalysis in the study of criminality, arguing that punishment of the forensic patient remains, in fact, a sheer waste of time. With foresight, Judge Westwick queried, "Can we not, in our well nigh hopeless and overwhelming struggle with the problems of delinquency and crime, profit by medical experience with the problems of health and disease? Will we not, eventually, terminate the senseless policy of sitting idly by until misbehavior occurs, often with irreparable damage, then dumping the delinquent into the juvenile court or reformatory and dumping the criminal into prison?" (p. 281). Westwick noted that we should, instead, train judges, probation officers, social workers, as well as teachers and parents, in the precepts of psychoanalysis, in order to arrive at a more sensitive, non-punitive understanding of the nature of criminality. He opined: "When we shall have succeeded in committing society to such a program, when we see it launched definitely upon the venture, as in time it surely will be—then shall we have erected an appropriate memorial to Sigmund Freud" (p. 281).

In more recent years, the field of forensic psychotherapy has become increasingly well constellated. Building upon the pioneering contributions of such psychoanalysts and psychotherapists as Edward Glover, Grace Pailthorpe, Melitta Schmideberg, and more recently Murray Cox, Mervin Glasser, Ismond Rosen, Estela Welldon, and others too numerous to mention, forensic psychotherapy has now become an increasingly formalized discipline that can be dated to the inauguration of the International Association for Forensic Psychotherapy and to the first annual conference, held at St. Bartholomew's Hospital in London in 1991. The profession now boasts a more robust foundation, with training courses developing in the United Kingdom and beyond. Since the inauguration of the Diploma in Forensic Psychotherapy (and subsequently the Diploma in Forensic Psychotherapeutic Studies), under the auspices of the British Postgraduate Medical Federation of the University of London in association with the Portman Clinic, students can now seek further instruction in the psychodynamic treatment of patients who act out in a dangerous and illegal manner.

The volumes in this series of books will aim to provide both practical advice and theoretical stimulation for introductory students and for senior practitioners alike. In the Karnac Books Forensic Psychotherapy Monograph Series, we will endeavour to produce a regular stream of high-quality titles, written by leading members of the profession, who will share their expertise in a concise and practice-orientated fashion. We trust that such a collection of books will help to consolidate the knowledge and experience that we have already acquired and will also provide new directions for the upcoming decades of the new century. In this way, we shall hope to plant the seeds for a more rigorous, sturdy, and wide-reaching profession of forensic psychotherapy.

As the new millennium begins to unfold, we now have an opportunity for psychotherapeutically orientated forensic mental health professionals to work in close conjunction with child psychologists and with infant mental health specialists so that the problems of violence can be tackled both preventatively and retrospectively. With the growth of the field of forensic psychotherapy, we at last have reason to be hopeful that serious criminality can be forestalled and perhaps, one day, even eradicated.

References

Bertin, C. (1982). *La Dernière Bonaparte*. Paris: Librairie Académique Perrin.

deMause, L. (1974). The evolution of childhood. In: Lloyd deMause (Ed.), *The History of Childhood* (pp. 1–73). New York: Psychohistory Press.

Kahr, B. (1994). The historical foundations of ritual abuse: an excavation of ancient infanticide. In: Valerie Sinason (Ed.), *Treating Survivors of Satanist Abuse* (pp. 45–56). London: Routledge.

Klein, M. (1932). *The Psycho-Analysis of Children*, trans. Alix Strachey. London: Hogarth Press and The Institute of Psycho-Analysis. [First published as *Die Psychoanalyse des Kindes*. Vienna: Internationaler Psychoanalytischer Verlag.]

Moellenhoff, F. (1966). Hanns Sachs, 1881–1947: the creative unconscious. In: F. Alexander, S. Eisenstein, & M. Grotjahn (Eds.), *Psychoanalytic Pioneers* (pp. 180–199). New York: Basic Books.

Nunberg, H., & Federn, E. (Eds.) (1962). *Minutes of the Vienna Psychoanalytic Society. Volume I: 1906–1908*, trans. Margarethe Nunberg. New York: International Universities Press.

Westwick, A. (1940). Criminology and Psychoanalysis. *Psychoanalytic Quarterly, 9*: 269–282.

ABOUT THE AUTHORS

Robert Bor has worked as both a clinical and academic psychologist, and also holds a pilot's licence. He is at present a consultant clinical psychologist at the Royal Free Hospital, London. He is Visiting Professor at City University, London where he teaches on the MSc in Air Transport Management and Emeritus Professor of Psychology at London Metropolitan University. He also contributes to the Diploma in Travel Health and Medicine at the Royal Free and University College Medical School in the Academic Department of Travel Medicine and Vaccines. He is a Chartered Clinical, Counselling and Health Psychologist and a Fellow of the British Psychological Society. He is a UKCP-Registered Family Therapist, having completed his specialist training at the Tavistock Clinic, London. He provides a specialist consultation service for air crew and their families for several leading international airlines and is also involved in the selection of airline pilots. He provides a treatment service for passengers who have a fear of flying at the Royal Free Travel Health Clinic in London. He has also served as an expert witness in aviation legal cases, relating to air rage, post incident traumatic stress reactions and crew behaviour. He serves on the editorial board of numerous leading international academic journals and has authored and co-authored several textbooks including: *Passenger Behaviour* (2003); *Psychological Perspectives on Fear of Flying* (2003); and *Doing Therapy Briefly* (2003) while the *Handbook of Pilot Mental Health* is due to be published in 2005. He is a Fellow of the Royal Aeronautical Society and a Member of the European Association for Aviation Psychology, the British Travel Health Association, and the Guild of Air Pilots and Air Navigators. He is also a member of the Association for Family Therapy, the Institute of Family Therapy, London, the American Association for Marital & Family Therapy, the American Psychological Association, and the American Family Therapy Academy. Robert Bor is a Churchill Fellow.

BRETT KAHR is Senior Clinical Research Fellow in Psychotherapy and Mental Health at the Centre for Child Mental Health in London, as well as Senior Lecturer in Psychotherapy in the School of Psychotherapy and Counselling at Regent's College. Since 2001 he has been the inaugural Winnicott Clinic Senior Research Fellow in Psychotherapy. He is the author or editor of several books, including *D.W. Winnicott: A Biographical Portrait*, which won the Gradiva Prize for Biography in 1997; *Forensic Psychotherapy and Psychopathology: Winnicottian Perspectives; Exhibitionism*; and *The Legacy of Winnicott: Essays in Infant and Child Mental Health*. A psychotherapist and marital psychotherapist in private practice, he serves as the Series Editor of the Forensic Psychotherapy Monograph Series for Karnac Books.

JANE N. ZUCKERMAN is a medical doctor and is Director of the WHO Collaborating Centre for Travel Medicine, the Academic Centre for Travel Medicine & Vaccines, and the Royal Free Travel Health Centre, Royal Free & University College Medical School.

FOREWORD

Jane N. Zuckerman

The speciality of travel medicine has evolved rapidly through the increase to hundreds of millions of people who travel between countries and across continents, by population movements and migration during the last few decades; consequently, the need has arisen to meet the health requirements of the diverse group who encompass travellers. Air travel has been facilitated by the development and increase in size of aircraft and of seating capacity, safety, and comfort, the affordable low air fares, and increasing business travel and tourism, since almost any place in the world can be reached within 24–36 hours. It is estimated that a billion people worldwide will soon travel by air at least once each year.

Aviation medicine is thus a vitally important topic, and aviation psychology forms an essential and integral part of travel medicine. While the origin of aviation psychology lies with the selection, psychological profile, mental health, and training and well-being of civilian and military pilots, this discipline has been vastly expanded by the imperative need to understand passenger behaviour as well.

This volume on clinical aerospace psychology written by Robert Bor, a clinical psychologist with unrivalled expertise in the subject, is a very welcome contribution to the speciality of travel medicine. The book covers comprehensively the mental health and psychology of pilots, including the psychological requirements for certification, environmental challenges, psychological problems among air crew, the effects of disruption to personal relationships, alcohol and drug misuse, pilot reactions to incidents and accidents, and the more recent and horrific topic of pilot suicide and terrorism by aircraft. Passenger behaviour receives no less comprehensive and excellent a discussion: including jet lag, fear of flying, air rage and behaviour during flight, the relationship between passengers and crew, and the often neglected impact on relationships of frequent travel.

This is a highly recommended, timely, and valuable contribution to travel health and medicine and essential reading for travel medicine physicians, psychologists, nurses, and specialists in occupational health as well as being of interest to those in the airline industry.

ANXIETY
AT 35,000 FEET

CHAPTER ONE

Towards the development of clinical aerospace psychology

On 11 September 2001, millions of people watched in horror as two commercial airliners crashed into the World Trade Center in New York City, one into the Pentagon in Washington, D.C., and a further one into a field in Pennsylvania. This constituted one of the most terrifying and audacious terrorist attacks experienced. Mental health professionals the world over could never have anticipated the psychological repercussions of such events. The images of the large commercial jets slamming into the sides of the Twin Towers—often replayed on television and reprinted in magazines and newspapers—have now become indelibly branded on our consciousness. Some clients and patients have discussed these events and their wider implications with trained therapists, and sometimes, too, with a new quality of anxiety.

It is reasonable to assume that every psychotherapeutic encounter has become affected by recent world events in a number of different ways. For many people, the terrorist attacks have aroused previously palpable feelings of insecurity and lack of safety that might have emerged in therapeutic work in other ways. Others who had been seasoned travellers have now developed an overt phobic reaction, or a fear of flying.

For those of us working in the mental health profession, we have become quite used to the notion that a fear of flying is irrational—something experienced by phobic and anxious personalities. Several decades ago, this problem might have been ascribed to those with "histrionic personalities". We now find ourselves on the cusp of revising this position, because it may be that in spite of statistical reassurance about the safety of air travel, none of us can be certain of this reassurance any more.

Some readers—even mental health professionals themselves—may be surprised to learn that psychologists and psychotherapists have been closely associated with the airline industry for many years, working to support and consulting to passengers, aircrew, and airlines. This speciality is known as "clinical aerospace psychology". We felt that the time is now ripe to better publicize this speciality, in the hope of making help better available and to further enlist the cooperation of mental health colleagues from cognate divisions of the psychological professions.

Psychologists working in the field of aerospace have concentrated, by and large, on certain ergonomic aspects of psychological consultation to the airline industry. They have, for example, developed better physical working conditions for pilots, improved the layout of the flight deck instruments, helped to eliminate potentially dangerous ambiguity in the communication between air traffic controllers and pilots, and taught crews how to operate more safely through Crew Resource Management (CRM). They have also studied the effects of jet lag in order to advise how best to mitigate against the unpleasant effects. A sub-speciality within aerospace psychology is clinical aerospace psychology, which is concerned with the mental aspects of aviation, and the insights are typically applied to helping to understand the behaviour of crew, passengers, maintenance personnel, air traffic controllers, and others involved in commercial and military aviation (Bor, 2003a; Bor & Van Gerwen, 2003).

Air travel, together with the aerospace industry, constitutes one of the world's largest industries. Yet, it was only a little over

100 years ago—on 17 December 1903, on a bitterly cold day—that the Wright brothers flew a distance of 120 feet in twelve seconds from the dunes at Kill Devil Hills in Ohio, heralding the age of modern flight. They could not have imagined the subsequent developments in aviation and space exploration that followed over the last century, which have been both rapid and stunning. Air travel affects so many aspects of our lives and how we able to relate, although these developments are now largely taken for granted. However, flight directly challenges our evolutionary capabilities because, as a species, we have not evolved naturally to fly. While most travellers appear to adapt to the physical and psychological demands of modern air travel, various penalties may be exacted in the course of doing so, and some may suffer from jet lag, a fear of flying, or travel stress. For a proportion, air travel poses an insurmountable challenge that may present in clinical settings. Until recently, a deeper understanding of these and related problems associated with air travel had not been readily available to mental health practitioners. This book seeks to remedy this in relation to certain key areas of practice.

Some of the other areas that are considered in the everwidening arena of clinical aerospace psychology include: psychological treatment for fear of flying, helping passengers to cope with the disrupted attachments that occur as a result of boarding an aeroplane, assisting the aircrew in the management of their own fears and anxieties inherent in their job situation, as well as contributing their expertise to the selection of aircrew (pilots and cabin crew). Readers who require an understanding of the physiological and health-related aspects of air travel should consult Jane Zuckerman's (2001) excellent book on the topic. In the safety-conscious climate of the modern era, there is also in certain cases a behind-the-scenes profiling of passengers. Psychologists are also concerned with developing ways to help airport managers and ground crew to become better resourced in their work to ensure greater job satisfaction and safety. An important further role is to provide post-incident counselling to survivors, family members, crew, and other employees who have become involved in airline incidents and disasters. We also

know that long-haul, transmeridian air travel can often exacerbate previously existing mental health disorders, and, thus, the
diagnosis and treatment of such individuals will become an
increasingly important area for mental health practitioners to
consider (Jauhar & Weller, 1982). Returning travellers are also at
increased risk of psychiatric illness due to a multitude of problems, ranging from homesickness and not coping well with
change to the side effects of antimalarials and the effects of illicit
drug use, among many possible triggers (Beny, Paz, & Potasman, 2001).

Many airline and military pilots regard the potential value of
psychology as quite risible. This deep scepticism towards psychologists stems, perhaps, in large measure from the long-standing historical use of psychometric testing in both the initial
selection of pilots for training and, later, in job promotion. Some
airline workers hold a rather narrow notion of the breadth and
scope of the mental health profession, and it is hoped that this
concise book will help to better explain the role of the clinical
aerospace psychologist or psychotherapist. Especially in an industry that privileges physical safety and robustness of pilots,
airline workers may be loath, in such a machismo community, to
seek professional help for mental health difficulties or anxieties
and, understandably, regard mental health workers with suspi-
cion. In a profit-driven industry, mental health welfare tends to
be marginalized and regarded as a luxury, unless a pilot becomes overtly depressed or alcoholic. Airlines have not been
particularly knowledgeable about or sensitive to brewing
stresses in their employees.

It is axiomatic that aviation involves extensive teamwork. As
psychologists and psychotherapists, we can draw on the enormous amount of research and clinical experience about the
dynamics of group interactions that we can bring to bear to the
aviation industry (Foushee, 1984). Our knowledge of difficulties
stemming from small-group interaction, sibling rivalry, complications arising from hierarchical interactions, and so forth, can
all help to shed light on what might occur on the flight deck and
among passenger–crew relationships.

Finally, whereas previous advertising for air travel concentrated on the leisure and pleasure of flying, our current preoccupations will be with safety and low-cost air travel. Airlines will have to face the problem of coping with new advertising strategies. This will be an arena in which psychologists might make a further important contribution, assisting the airline advertisers to become increasingly sensitive to the fears that are experienced by millions of contemporary airline travellers worldwide.

The aim in preparing this short book is to introduce mental health practitioners to the basic concepts of clinical aerospace psychology, with a primary emphasis on psychotherapeutic and clinical psychological issues that may present among passengers and aircrew, rather than those of ergonomics, which have previously dominated this arena. Readers are provided with an up-to-date and condensed account of current practices and issues in this burgeoning and increasingly important speciality within psychology. A variety of inter-related topics are explored, ranging from the mental health of airline pilots to the causes and treatments of travel phobias. Some overt psychological recommendations are also given for ways in which mental health workers might improve the psychological well-being of those who fly on planes. Some of the issues raised will be able to impact directly on efficiency, safety, and security in the airline industry.

One aim in preparing this book has been to avoid, wherever possible, psychological jargon, to which our profession has become so increasingly prone, so that this book may be profitably enjoyed by both mental health colleagues and those who work in the airline industry. We hope that the book will also be of use to those colleagues who do not anticipate developing their expertise further in the field of clinical aerospace psychology, but who nonetheless seek a deeper understanding of some of the issues. Some of these will be working with clients or patients who bring their travel-related fears and phobias (whether rational or irrational) into the clinical consulting room. The remainder of the book provides an overview of some of the main current issues and psychological perspectives relating to these broad topics.

CHAPTER TWO

Understanding passenger behaviour

A ir travel has never been so accessible to travellers. An estimated one billion people worldwide make at least one plan trip each year. Unfortunately, the dream of flight nurtured by Leonardo da Vinci and the Wright brothers is sometimes tarnished by stress and anxiety. Less than four decades ago, air travel was exciting, attracting a small number of the elite and wealthy passengers, and although sometimes dangerous, it was usually a great adventure that enabled people to travel at greater speeds than ever before. Passengers were both pampered and obedient. The advent of large commercial aircraft in the 1960s, in an industry of mass air transportation, and cheap accessible flights has changed all this. Airline advertisements continue to raise expectations among air travellers, because the product being promoted is still being perceived as glamorous. Disappointment sets in when expectations are not met, and high levels of stress may be one outcome.

Man has not naturally evolved to fly, as the psychologist, James Reason reminded us (1974). Even though as a species we have evolved over millions of years, our bodies are largely still designed to hunt and gather in small groups, probably on the plains of Africa. We remain a species that is best designed and equipped to be self-propelling at a few miles per hour in two dimensions under the conditions of terrestrial gravity (Reason, 1974). There are several obstacles and "physical evolution barriers" to our position or motion senses, as well as our capacity for processing information, that is apparent to both the novice air traveller and the most seasoned pilot. While there have been remarkable achievements in engineering over the past century that have made air travel both possible and highly accessible within the span of a single lifetime, this has not been without its challenges. When evolutionary barriers to motion are exceeded, numerous penalties are exacted, the most common of which are motion sickness, jet lag, and increased arousal and stress. For flight crew, there may be additional problems related to judgement, decision-making, perception, and concentration, among others. Air travel often brings us into close contact with strangers, and an understanding of the social psychology of behaviour within groups and teams is relevant. Emerging problems, such as the advent of larger commercial aircraft and flying greater distances non-stop, are likely to become increasingly challenging in years to come. Air travel disrupts human relationships and behaviours, as well as bodily functions and systems.

Stress may begin long before passengers set out for the airport: making travel arrangements, preparing to leave home, and saying goodbye to family, friends, or colleagues can all increase stress and distress. Frequent air travel may also disrupt relationships. Psychologists have studied relationship dynamics among both aircrew and passengers and examined attachment patterns in "intermittent spouse" relationships, by which is meant disruption to enduring personal relationships by the comings and goings of the frequent traveller—whether businessperson or pilot. In one study, attachment behaviour in adults (measured by avoidance and anxiety levels) and symptoms of emotional distress (e.g. insomnia, emotional upset, feelings of isolation) were found to be affected by relationship status, length, and strength, with anxiously attached partners displaying or suffering greater distress (Fraley & Shaver, 1998). Crowds at airports, or the close proximity of fellow travellers on board aircraft, coupled with noise, apprehension about travel, fatigue, hunger, emotional arousal due to separation from a loved one, as well as language and communication difficulties can test even the most resilient and healthy of air travellers.

Most passengers have expectations about travel, and these may be built around punctuality, quality of service, or amenities available at airports or on board aircraft. Many travellers will attempt to cope with the anxiety of flying by relying upon what psychoanalysts refer to as "transitional objects" or comforters, such as magazines and sweets, a personal stereo, alcohol, and so forth, as familiar sources of pleasure to ease the stress of separation from *terra firma*. When little sources of comfort (such as a chicken dinner instead of beef or a sufficiently warm towel to wipe one's face) are not provided, then primitive distress may ensue.

There are times when passengers' expectations are not met, due to delays or poor service. These may be predictable, but they are no less annoying as a result. We have learned that passengers react differently to stress. Some resort to alcohol ingestion to relieve boredom, anxiety, or irritation. Others become militant about what they believe to be their rights, and they may become insistent or hostile towards ground staff or cabin crew. Another sub-group of passengers become quite withdrawn or servile, enduring things that they would not do ordinarily. Still others reach for medication to reduce anxiety or to induce sleep. Paradoxically, some of these coping strategies may further aggravate the situation and increase stress, as they directly effect people's behaviour, their ability to cope with demanding situations, and their cognitive abilities in general.

In view of all the potential disruption to one's lifestyle at 35,000 feet, even the well-heeled traveller who flies frequently will find himself or herself in both physically and emotionally unfamiliar territory, and this setting can readily prime the individual to become anxious and irascible. Each air traveller must develop his or her own strategies to make the journey more manageable. As psychologists, we have a role to play in educating passengers about what some of the anxieties might be, so that these fears can be made more conscious, rather than simmering away unconsciously (Bor, 2003a).

Fear of flying

For some passengers, the ordinary anxieties of travelling reach more insidious levels and can come to constitute a constellation of symptomatology known formally as "fear of flying". A fear of flying ranges from minor and usually transient apprehension at one end of the scale, either in anticipation of or during an actual flight, which does little more than cause the smallest amounts of psychological turbulence and which soon disappears. At the other end of the scale, one can be presented with a full-blown phobic reaction, which can even result in a breakdown at an airport, with the potential passenger in hysterics and tears, vomiting, and even refusing to board the aeroplane. Some of these people will, in fact, never have boarded an aircraft. As Mark Twain remarked, many anxious people spend their lives "suffering from tragedies that never occur".

While there is an increasing amount of published literature on the psychological treatment of fear of flying (e.g. Bor & Van Gerwen, 2003), many unanswered questions remain about the causes, classification/diagnosis, epidemiology, and spectrum of symptoms of the problem. In DSM-III-R (APA, 1987), fear of flying was listed and defined as a simple phobia. Subsequently, as with many other psychological disorders, this conceptualization was revised. In DSM-IV, fear of flying was placed in the category of specific phobias (APA, 1994). This is not, however, entirely helpful to either the clinician or the researcher. A fear of flying can be a sub-category or main category of one or more other phobias, such as claustrophobia and a fear of confinement. Equally, a fear of flying may be a symptom of the effect of generalization of another phobia that is common in certain environmental conditions described in DSM-IV (APA, 1994), such as a fear of heights, instability, or falling, among others. Understandably, mental health practitioners—both clinicians and researchers—sometimes disagree over the diagnosis and classification of fear of flying.

Psychologists can measure the fear of flying with a certain amount of objectivity through the use of standardized psychometric tests specifically developed for this purpose (Van Gerwen, Spinhoven, Van Dyck, & Diekstra, 1999). Although some people score much more highly on these tests than do others, even those reporting only a mild fear of flying should be treated seriously by mental health professionals, as the suffering is relative from person to person. Furthermore, as has already been pointed out, a fear of flying may also be a symptom of another underlying psychological problem.

Two questions emerge—namely, what causes a fear of flying, and why is everyone not affected in the same way when presented with the same potential threat? There are several different causes of the fear of flying, and the main ones are listed below:

1. *Lack of familiarity.* The person is certain that if he or she flies, the plane will crash, and death will follow. The patient looks at the plane and surmises that given its weight and structure, it cannot possibly be supported or lifted by moving air. Patients also fail to understand or to accept that air traffic controllers maintain separation between aircraft, and that pilots can still land the plane, even in conditions of poor visibility. People are distressed by any unfamiliar sounds in the aircraft cabin, or turning motions. They scrutinize the crew's faces for indications that something is terribly wrong and seldom leave their seat during flight. These people often have large gaps in their knowledge of how planes fly, or have distorted the information of safety statistics and information that is available.

2. *Past experiences.* Previous experiences of delays, turbulence, or of aborted take-offs or landings may instil fear that becomes more pronounced when the person has to go on another journey. This is in spite of the fact that the person has already survived an unpleasant experience. The fear is that it

will be repeated, or worse. Past traumatic experiences may or may not be linked to a fear of flying, and are therefore always worthy of further exploration.

3. *Lack of control.* Air travel involves placing trust in other skilled professionals. Almost every aspect of the experience reinforces a sense of lack of control: we queue, wait, have to check in, are separated from luggage, may be delayed, are told when we are to be seated and when we may leave our seats, and so on. Feeling that we have little control in the situation and associated feelings of being infantilized can increase feelings of anxiety. People prone to suffering panic attacks also fear that they will lose control of their body. Some even welcome a crash to end the extreme unpleasant-ness of a full-blown panic attack.

4. *Claustrophobia.* This is a fear of being trapped in a small or confined space, and aircraft cabins are environments that are primed to produce such a response. As soon as passengers hear the captain instructing the cabin crew to "set the doors to automatic and cross check", all prospect of escape disap-pears: after all, one cannot simply ask the pilot to pull over, as one might do if one is riding in a car and having a panic attack.

5. *Acrophobia.* This is a fear of heights, and it may also, there-fore, be associated with a fear of flying. The person is terrified of the prospect of the thousands of feet of "empty space" between the ground and the plane. The patient does not trust the environment, which is perceived as fragile, and fears falling from a very great height. Some of those who suffer from acrophobia and yet still manage to board an aircraft often fear moving around the cabin, because they believe that they will disturb the movement of the plane or unbalance it by moving about, or that they might even fall through the floor.

6. *Negative and catastrophic thinking.* A person suffering from low mood or depression, or someone who has experienced a recent adverse life event such as a death, break-up of a relationship, or loss of a job, may experience negative emo-

tions that become highly exacerbated in the non-neutral situation of flying on an aeroplane. The individual may not actually recognize the association between the stressful life events and the fear: consequently they start to worry about worrying, and all their psychological distress becomes increasingly compounded. Patients will focus on the fact that they also have a new symptom—namely, a fear of flying. In a stress-susceptible personality, the fear may stem from low self-esteem, a low inability to take risks, perfectionism, or a tendency towards catastrophic thinking about everyday events. Those who are prone to catastrophize are likely to be more susceptible to negative thinking. The trigger for unleashing unpleasant thoughts or even a panic attack can sometimes be traced to specific crew communications in the aircraft cabin. An example is the cabin crew safety demonstration, sometimes prefaced with: "In the unlikely event . . .". This and other cues apparently induce anxiety in some individuals who feel doomed to a tragic fate over which they feel they have no control.

7. *Heredity as a pre-disposing factor.*   There is an increased risk of having fears and suffering from anxiety and panic attacks when other family members have been previously affected, and this may be due to a genetic link or learned behaviour where events in a shared environment might condition the person to a particular response or reaction to stress.

8. *Childhood environment.*   This can give rise to a range of fears, one of which may be associated with flying. Parents may be over-protective or controlling, or they may set impossibly high standards from which self-doubt and fear may arise. In later life, these may lead to a fear of flying.

This list is by no means exhaustive, and psychologists recognize that a fear of flying can result from a combination of several of these possible causes, as well as others not mentioned. One symptom of fear is avoidance, and while this defence mechanism is sometimes helpful, it is unlikely to lead to a cure of the problem. Using certain prescribed medications or recreational drugs to mask the problem sometimes makes it worse because of the effect that such stimulants may have during and after the situation.

Psychological assessment and treatment of fear of flying

Relative to other phobias, a fear of flying affects a large proportion of the population, and it affects up to 20% of airline passengers at any one time (Iljon Foreman & Borrill, 1994). Similarly to other phobias, a fear of flying is unlikely to disappear without treatment, as each time the patient avoids flying, the phobia is liable to become more entrenched and the symptoms more severe. Patients may ask their doctor or nurse to treat the phobia pharmacologically and therefore provide a medical solution to what is essentially a psychological problem with physiological manifestations. This section describes a psychological approach to the treatment of fear of flying derived from evidence-based treatment methods (Bor & Van Gerwen, 2003).

Patients who present with a fear of flying may identify flight anxiety directly when they request treatment for flight phobia. Alternatively, a fear of flying may be demonstrated through indirect consequences of symptoms that may impinge on other aspects of their lives. For example, it may present where it causes difficulties in relationships, inhibiting career progression, or through incidents of so-called "air rage" through excessive alcohol use (Bor, 1999). A fear of flying should not be lightly dismissed by health care professionals, as the effects can wreak havoc in people's lives and the fear may also be indicative of a more general anxiety disorder. Flight phobics may present to health-care professionals with symptoms that initially indicate a simple association between anxiety and the experience of flying. However, certain features of a fear of flying must be considered, and these are most relevant in the assessment stage. Flight phobia differs from other "simple" phobias in that it is considered to be a constellation of four fundamental fears: fear of heights, fear of crashing, fear of instability, and fear of confinement. Around 46% of travellers with a fear of flying also have other phobias; some 33% of these travellers commonly present with agoraphobia, and some 25% with claustrophobia (Dean & Whitaker, 1982). In addition, other events and factors in the person's life that cause stress, such as relationship problems or redundancy, can increase their susceptibility to anxiety (Doctor, McVarish, & Boone, 1990).

Health care professionals should ensure that they make a full assessment of the patient's situation in general, as well as specific information relevant to the implementation of systematic desensitization treatments. Information of general relevance may include:

The psychological histories of travellers and their families. Given that most phobias can be acquired through vicarious learning and modelling, the behaviour of primary carers in relation to the fear stimulus should be identified, as well as the coping strategies that they commonly employ.

Personality factors. Individuals who have a high degree of emotional reactivity are more at risk of acquiring phobias. As such, introverts have been shown to be more prone to conditioning and may acquire fear of flying more quickly or to a greater degree.

Psychiatric factors. Particular attention should be paid to travellers who have a psychiatric diagnosis. For example, treatment of a patient with fear of flying who also suffers from a borderline personality disorder must include very close monitoring for progress and relapse. An evaluation of the patient's emotional stability and level of cognitive functioning must be made prior to treatment.

Standardized tests. Such tests can provide accurate information about the nature and degree of the fear of flying. The Flight Anxiety Situations Questionnaire (Van Gerwen et al., 1999) determines the degree of anxiety experienced in different situations associated with air travel. The Flight Anxiety Modality Questionnaire (Van Gerwen et al, 1999) differentiates between cognitive and somatic symptoms of the fear of flying.

The reasons for which a traveller seeks treatment at this particular time can provide a useful indication of the anxiety components specific to the individual's fear of flying. When making a behavioural assessment for systematic desensitization treatment, information should be obtained that relates to the following areas:

1. determining the target behaviours to be changed and the maintaining factors;

2. ascertaining the patient's social and personal resources, as well as their coping skills (the aim is to capitalize on useful strategies, and, where appropriate, to introduce more appropriate skills; also, factors that may limit and/or inhibit treatment must be identified);

3. identifying those interventions that are most likely to be adopted by the patient, according to their particular circumstances.

Flight phobic travellers may require a package of treatments where the emphasis may or may not be on their fears about flying and may address other external factors. All treatments should, however, be directed towards improving the traveller's ability to manage their anticipatory anxiety as well as those fears that they encounter at airports and on board the aircraft.

The most widely accepted psychological explanation for the acquisition of the fear of flying comes from the classical conditioning paradigm. Anxiety is considered to be a response that is learned when a "danger signal" is perceived. The "danger signal" is previously paired with a situation that naturally produces a negative reaction through direct exposure, modelling, or vicarious learning. The individual will, through a process of operant conditioning, behave in a way that will either reduce anxiety levels or achieve a state of safety. The fear of flying, in common with most phobias, is viewed as a form of aversive conditioning, maintained by avoidance behaviours.

People who suffer from a fear of flying commonly present with a number of symptoms that are either related to their thoughts, behaviours, physiology, or social circumstances. These symptoms can occur at any stage from anticipating the journey to the airport to returning home. Individuals with flight phobia frequently have negative thoughts associated with air travel and have a tendency to amplify or catastrophize the level of threat posed by certain aspects of flying. They commonly experience anxiety symptoms when they anticipate the flight or are unable to avoid a flight. The physical symptoms of flight anxiety include breathlessness, sweating, palpitations, diarrhoea, dry mouth, tension, nausea, tightness in the throat, and even feeling faint. Flight phobics invariably become preoccupied with ways to avoid flying when faced with the prospect of air travel, actively plan alternatives, and seek to minimize the likelihood of having to take the trip. This can have significant consequences for the individual's personal and professional life: for example, avoidance may prevent them progressing in their career or lead to problems in their relationships when planning a family holiday.

Psychological interventions are typically designed to introduce new information about the situation, with the aim of increasing the individual's perception of their ability to cope or altering their appraisal of the situation as threatening. Those interventions designed to increase the individual's ability to cope are usually aimed at their physiological reactions to the threat and include relaxation training, thought stopping, and stress inoculation training. Interventions designed to decrease the appraisal of threat are most commonly directed towards the traveller's thoughts about flying and their coping behaviours. A reduction in threat appraisal can be achieved by providing information about the experience, increased exposure to air travel, through the use of virtual reality training programmes (Rothbaum, Hodges, Smith, Lee, & Price, 2000), and through cognitive restructuring of the traveller's beliefs about flying.

Typically, however, many cognitive behavioural therapy intervention packages are applied inflexibly and may therefore not suit and benefit all those who seek treatment. A proportion may require interventions only in one single area—such as providing information about how aeroplanes fly and do not collide with each other in the sky, or skills to manage anticipatory anxiety or relaxation training. It is important, therefore, that mental health workers make a thorough assessment of the nature of the person's fear of flying and pay particular attention both to the onset and to the maintenance of the phobia in order to develop the most appropriate and focused interventions.

Interventions aimed at evaluating the perceived threat have the additional psychological benefit of helping to maintain the individual's perception of effective coping in feared situations in general, which is referred to as "self-efficacy" (Bandura, 1977). This improves the patient's confidence and sense of control over critical factors in the feared situation. Control is a particularly important in flight phobias, as travellers tend to place control over the situation externally (Borrill & Iljon Foreman, 1996), and this is frequently associated with stress. In the case of fear of flying, control may relate to the person's physiological symptoms, actions, and/or thoughts. What can follow from that is that treatment for flight phobia will help to facilitate the traveller's reappraisal of the threat of those aspects of flying that evoke anxiety. This is achieved through three main types of intervention:

1. education about the physical principles of flight and the process by which the flight crew control the aircraft;
2. experiential learning through participating in a simulated or actual flight situation;
3. training and techniques to manage the physiological symptoms of anxiety.

Few people will ever have witnessed the actual event of an aircraft crash, though the aftermath may fill the pages of newspapers or television screens. The psychological impact of the events of 11 September 2001 is likely to be complex and far-reaching. The images of civilian airliners being flown into the World Trade Center, and the realization later that the normal use of a safe and popular form of transportation had been perversely turned into a weapon of mass destruction, is disturbing to even the seasoned air traveller. While air travel has arguably become safer since these events, it will take some time before commercial aviation returns to "normal"—if ever. The reason for this is that our initial responses to the perceived threat associated with flying have less to do with logic and a rational appraisal of how safe it is to fly, but more with the disturbing images, from which we naturally recoil and withdraw psychologically. Before 11 September, most psychological intervention programmes regarded the patient's fear of being involved in an accident as, at best, an irrational fear, and, at worst, an almost a perverse fantasy. Nowadays, in light of recent terrorist attacks, well-publicized accidents, and even a few pilot suicides, therapeutic conversations will need to take better cognizance of the improbable though realistic possibility of mortality. In other words, it would be insensitive for a therapist to dismiss out of hand a patient's fear that he or she will die in an aircraft accident and, at the very least, might need to address those feelings associated with separation, coping with uncertainty, and death.

The most commonly used intervention is systematic desensitization developed by Wolpe (1958), and it is based upon the principle of reciprocal inhibition, where a response that is incompatible with anxiety is evoked at the time when the fear reaction ordinarily occurs. Most treatments use relaxation training to evoke a calm response to substitute for the anxiety reaction. Treatments using systematic desensitization tend to follow a standard protocol: first, the patient is counselled about relaxation techniques; this is followed by the creation of an anxiety hierarchy and then by systematic desensitization proper (Wolpe, 1958). The intervention may include either direct exposure, by asking the traveller to experience the situation "live", or indirect exposure, where the traveller is asked to picture the feared situation using guided imagination techniques.

The anxiety hierarchy is developed by first asking patients to describe different situations associated with the phobia, which evoke an anxiety response. The degree to which the client is able to imagine a situation can also be determined at this point to indicate whether or not exposure techniques will be effective. By writing these situations on index cards, the patient can then organize the cards according to how the degree—on a scale of 1 to 100 (where 100 denotes extreme anxiety)—to which they rate each situation as anxiety-provoking. The patient is asked to provide between 15 and 20 situations, which may include, for example, leaving a partner, going through passport control, waiting at the departure gate, and entering the aircraft. At this stage, it is important to ensure that those antecedents that evoke anxiety are explicit and the descriptions of the stimuli are realistic.

During desensitization proper, the patient is first helped to achieve a state of deep relaxation and then asked to imagine the scene that produces the least anxiety, and themselves within it, for 20 seconds. It is important to ensure that the patient is given the opportunity to signal when their anxiety levels become intolerable and a situation that evokes a lower level of fear should be used or the period of exposure should be reduced. When the situation no longer evokes anxiety, the patient then addresses the next situation. This process is repeated until the patient has been successfully exposed to all the situations in the hierarchy without the fear reaction being evoked. The total length of treatment can depend on the number of situations identified by the patient and any factors that may interfere with the treatment process, such as external life stressors or personality factors. All treatments should aim ultimately to include "live" exposure to the fear situation adopting the same strategy for desensitization as with exposure using imagination.

As is common with many other interventions for psychological problems, treatment can be enhanced with the use of selected medication, such as beta-blockers. This can be of particular importance where the traveller's physiological reaction is so intense that it prevents the psychological treatment from having any effect. Medication can also be effective in complementing anxiety management and relaxation techniques, allowing the traveller to inhibit their avoidance response and gain new information to re-evaluate the situation as non-threatening.

The efficacy of treatment programmes has been examined to determined whether the successes that are reported in treatment are maintained over time and whether different treatment components between programmes are more likely to predict lasting change, and what the traveller's anxiety levels are. Programmes that include behavioural interventions such as systematic desensitization and cognitive restructuring have an overall success rate of 88%, while the success of non-behavioural treatment programmes falls dramatically to 18% of travellers (Doctor, McVarish, & Boone, 1990). Long-term exploratory psychoanalytic therapy has not been shown to be effective, *per se*.

An important distinction arises between cognitive behavioural programmes that have used direct *in vivo* exposure compared to those only using exposure. Treatment involving direct exposure shows a significant reduction in anxiety levels over time (Roberts, 1989). However, if the programme requires travellers only to imagine the feared situation, then the reduction in fear achieved during treatment does not transfer to the actual flight, and consequently patients tend to have a higher relapse rate. Treatments, therefore, usually require a battery of interventions in order to help people to overcome both the symptoms and the underlying fears that give rise to them.

These are the core ingredients of the standard, traditional method for working with fear of flying, though not all mental health professionals will approach the matter in the same way. It might be helpful for the reader to have a clearer idea of the key therapeutic features that may be of value for the patient. At a recent international conference on the treatment of the fear of flying, held in Vienna, Austria, in November 2000, a group of specialists generated the following "Ten Golden Rules for Patients with Fear of Flying", most of which focus on cognitive and behavioural (somatic) hints for the patient:

- Motivation is the key to change.
- Keep flying, don't avoid it.
- Stop the "what ifs" and focus on "what is".
- Avoid caffeine, sugar, nicotine, and self-medication.
- Practice relaxation.
- Turbulence is uncomfortable, but safe when buckled up.

- Drink plenty of water and avoid alcohol; the latter has the effect of increasing fear and causes dehydration.
- Monitor your breathing and ensure that it remains rhythmic.
- Planes are designed and built to fly.
- Develop personal coping cards with reminders of what actually works for you.

This list of practical tips may be of some value to certain patients, although most readers would recognize that this cannot bring full reassurance. The same aviation psychology colleagues have also highlighted a number of useful concepts and ideas for working with clients or patients who struggle with flight phobias, including encouraging patients to take an active role in their psychological treatment by not denying the problem. They have also stressed the importance of helping patients to deal with thoughts and images about their specific fears associated with flying, and to learn to control physical responses to anxiety. It might also be helpful to educate patients about the ways in which fear becomes manifest psychosomatically in the body, as well as teach patients techniques for relaxation (Bor, Josse, & Palmer, 2000).

As we have seen, most patients suffering from fear of flying can be treated successfully. However, not all anxious or vulnerable individuals seek appropriate treatment: some manage to contain their anxieties and psychological distresses and actually board an aircraft. A proportion of these anxious passengers will remain fearful but subjugate their feelings and withdraw into themselves. It is only while airborne that, for a few, substantial enactment occurs, resulting in what have come to be called "in-flight psychiatric emergencies". As many as 3.5% of all in-flight medical emergencies are primarily of a psychiatric nature, and the vast majority of these are actually cases of acute anxiety. More worrying is the number of documented cases of actual psychoses aboard an aircraft (Beny, Paz, & Potasman, 2001; Matsumoto & Goebert, 2001). Psychiatric episodes are more likely to occur at specific points, especially during the latter part of a long flight; the other particularly vulnerable time occurs during the early morning hours of an overnight flight (Ekeberg, Kjeldsen, Greenwood, & Enger, 1990; Jauhar & Weller, 1982). Some three quarters of these documented emergencies presented in female passengers. It has been recommended that anxiolytic medication should be made available in the on-board medical kit in order to cope with such emergencies and to prevent disruption to other passengers.

Although it is not of direct relevance to airline passengers, readers might be interested to know that among people living close to airports, psychiatric hospital admission rates are associated with aircraft noise and living close to a major airport (Kryter, 1990).

Air rage and unruly passenger behaviour

Research into airline passenger behaviour has, until recently, been overlooked because it had been assumed that all passengers are compliant and adaptive to the unique demands of air travel (Bor, 2003a). However, the increase in the frequency and severity of disruptive passenger incidents—including recent deaths—has challenged this belief. As such, the safety implications of passenger behaviour have assumed greater significance and have come to dominate the aerospace psychology agenda. There are a number of factors that impinge upon the air traveller, each of which may directly or indirectly influence passenger behaviour. These factors include the quality of the travel experience and the traveller's ability to cope with potential stressors during the journey. For those who find managing the travel experience more difficult, their lack of effective coping is manifest in behaviours akin to the "fight-or-flight" response found in animals. The response is one directed towards either escape or attack in relation to the threatening situation. The lack of escape or avoidance possibilities on board an aircraft has resulted in "fight reactions" of aggression associated with high anxiety levels. Most incidents are directed at cabin staff, the most immediately accessible representatives of the airline, often regarded as parental figures who control passengers' access to food and toilets and so forth (Lane & Bor, 2002). These "powers" may be deeply resented by a passenger who has a prior grievance or sense of entitlement, or who may even be intoxicated. While it has always been accepted that a small proportion of passengers might be suffering from overt psychiatric problems and might become disruptive on aircraft, most perpetrators of air rage have not had psychiatric illness histories. The fact that the vast majority of airline passengers cope with and manage the pressures of modern air travel when exposed to identical stresses and potential triggers for acting-out behaviour suggests that certain personalities or categories of passenger may be predisposed to air rage. Current research is focusing on the association between air rage and a history of antisocial behaviour among perpetrators.

An air traveller's ability to manage his or her relationships with fellow passengers and crew is a crucial part of the travel experience, particularly where individual space is compromised. This is especially relevant where air passengers are likely to come into contact with people from other cultures or nationalities. Passengers are required to respond flexibly to the heterogeneity of different groups and different styles of communication. When passengers have a reduced capacity to cope, due to a lack of skills, knowledge, circadian desynchronization (jet lag), fatigue, disruption to eating patterns, a lack of empathy, or high levels of personal stress, their reactions may become more aggressive, as a result of extremes of frustration, and these people display a greater level of intolerance. This in turn may lead to anxious and fractious relationships with others.

The air traveller has to contend with a number of stressors that, cumulatively, may culminate in an episode of "acting out", and this includes aggressive and threatening behaviour and possibly both verbal and physical assault. Beginning with long queues for checking in at airports, separation from one's luggage, numerous security checks that might involve bodily checks, long walks to the departure lounge, negotiating crowds and the terrain of a large modern airport, passengers are subjected to numerous stresses even before they board an aircraft.

Once on board, the passenger may feel the need to compete for the armrest or the overhead locker as a territorial marker or to establish dominance over a fellow passenger who may be perceived as a threat or as an intruder in one's private space. Some passengers also may not be satisfied with the seating arrangements, often randomly allocated. They may sense de-individualization on the aircraft and be referred to as the "passenger in 34C". Cramped conditions on board aircraft may exacerbate stress and trigger acts of violence. Emotional reactions intensify and stress increases when personal space is invaded by strangers (Freedman, 1975; Rotten, 1987), although reactions may be mediated by culture and gender. Crowded and cramped conditions may lead to feelings of de-individuation, and this is found to be linked to less restrained behaviour (Diener, 1980).

Restlessness from excessive "seat-belts on" conditions, lengthy non-stop flights in cramped aircraft, sleep disturbance, claustrophobia, and the effects of certain prescribed or illicit drugs have been implicated in air rage incidents. Research has demonstrated that the unique environment of the aircraft cabin directly affects behaviour. The air inside an aircraft cabin is usually dry and low in humidity (Edwards & Edwards, 1990). Deviations in the aircraft cabin from usual ambient conditions have been found to produce stress and irritability, while lowered air pressure can lead to mild hypoxia and impairment of cognitive tasks such as reasoning (Bell, Greene, Fisher, & Baum, 1996; Denison, Ledwith, & Poulton, 1966). Noise levels from the engines and outside air rushing past the aircraft are an additional source of stress. Loud noise also leads to people having to raise their voices when communicating, which can be misconstrued as aggressive behaviour, thereby increasing tension between people (Bell et al., 1996). Flight crew share the same environment with passengers and are also affected by noise, low humidity, low air pressure, cramped working conditions, and fatigue, all of which may affect their performance, seat-side manner, alertness, and mood (Beh & McLaughlin, 1991).

Passengers may also be more emotionally aroused, which can intensify how they cope with stressful or unfamiliar situations. They may be anxious about being separated from a loved one, homesick, concerned about a business trip, upset that they cannot console a distressed child, lonely, or excited; they may even think about their spouse having an affair while they themselves are abroad. Some passengers, removed from their familiar surroundings, may believe that the rules that govern relationships on the ground do not apply at 35,000 feet. One often feels in "nowhere-land" and perhaps not subject to the laws of any particular country, perhaps more disinhibited, and thus, more likely to act out. For example:

- When denied another drink, an intoxicated first-class passenger (dubbed "patient zero" by those who study so-called cabin fever) proceeded to pull down his trousers and underpants and defecated on the cabin floor and also on the food trolley.

- On a flight out of Los Angeles, California, a passenger struck a flight attendant because he was told that there were no more chicken meals for dinner.

- A disgruntled passenger on another flight actually tried to throw a flight attendant out of an emergency exit.

- When asked to remove his headset while the aircraft was taxiing, a passenger struck a flight attendant so hard that he was sent flying into the next row of seats.

- After being denied an upgrade to first class, a passenger and his travelling companion threatened to "take the plane down". During the ensuing fracas to restrain the passenger, a flight attendant received second-degree burns from being scalded by hot coffee.

- A flight attendant was seriously injured by a passenger who hit her with a bottle of duty-free alcohol. She sustained injury requiring her to have over 30 stitches, and she could not return to her job.

Contrary to some popular wisdom, in-flight violence is not confined to economy-class passengers, who, it had been assumed, may be reacting to the crowded and cramped conditions. Anecdotal evidence suggests that business-class passengers and members of frequent flyer programmes can be extremely demanding and aggressive, as they have higher expectations of service, and may carry a greater sense of narcissistic entitlement (Dahlberg, 2001). It has been observed that passengers' behaviour during flight is directly linked to the stress they may experience in their life generally, as well as to the extent of emotional arousal associated with travel, and to the extent of potentially disrupted attachments. Passengers who experience difficulties at work, in their relationships, or with their physical health may be more prone to stress when flying and potentially more emotionally charged or aggressive.

Some airlines have recently taken certain steps to combat in-flight violence. British Airways now issues individual "warning cards" to unruly passengers from the captain, advising them that if they persist in their threatening behaviour, they will be prosecuted, and British Airways also teaches cabin crew how to restrain such passengers physically, if required. Passing down custodial sentences to offenders by the courts also conveys the message that in-flight violence will not be tolerated. However, for any deterrent to be effective, a would-be perpetrator must believe that there is a significant chance that they will be caught and that the consequences will be severe. This requires consistency in approach throughout the airline industry. Equally, no incident, however minor, must go unpunished. This amounts to a "zero-tolerance" strategy on every airline. This has certain limitations. In order to convict a passenger, crew members must be prepared to report the incident and give evidence. Pressure from colleagues not to delay an onward flight, problems understanding language, customs, and legal processes, as well as indifference on the part of police officers may deter crew from reporting incidents. In addition, "zero tolerance" places excessively high demands on crew, who themselves cannot afford to be culpable of any offence, however minor.

The dilemma this raises for airlines is that their response could have far-reaching consequences for customer relations. It could also backfire if it is proved that a crew member had a part to play in provoking a passenger or letting a situation get out of hand. Knowing that they have the backing and support of the airline behind them may encourage a crew member to escalate a simple customer service to dangerous proportions.

Airlines do not easily admit to complicity in this problem, yet it transpires that some incidents have been the result of a lethal combination: for example, a disgruntled passenger treated poorly at check-in who becomes inebriated on the flight and is served by an overworked or jet-lagged cabin-crew member. A seemingly minor trigger event—such as an unanticipated event or the non-availability of a special meal—has lead to verbal or physical violence. Air rage is most often the outcome of unique contextual factors, as well as a complex interactive sequence between the perpetrator and the victim, which may be governed by social rules and expectations, a sense of entitlement, and personality types (Bor, 2003b; Bor, Russell, Parker, & Papadopoulos, 2001).

Threatening behaviour and actual violence are occupational hazards that are by no means confined to flight attendants. Those who work in other service-based industries, members of the police force, and others whose job it is to intervene with anxious or disturbed people are frequently assaulted in the course of their work. Psychiatric social workers, nurses, and taxi drivers are high on the list of those who frequently face danger in their jobs. Employees require training and unique skills in order to cope with the threat of violence in the workplace. They also need to feel reassured that their organization has a clear policy about combating violence and that they will receive psychological and practical support from their employers should they become victims of a verbal or physical assault (Leather, Brady, Lawrence, Beale, & Cox, 1999).

The passenger–crew relationship

Acts of air rage are, however, probably more than an impulsive venting of fury. They may signal a worrying breakdown in the communications between the passengers and the flight crew.

Flight attendants may experience role confusion. Their principal role is to ensure passenger and cabin safety, yet the expectations of passengers are quite different. Cabin crew report that passengers are more interested in being pampered than in the important matter of safety.

An understanding of passenger behaviour is important in relation to flight safety and coping with and survivability of air accidents. As a result of improved safety measures that have been implemented over the years, the number of air accidents has steadily decreased. However, this has not been accompanied by a corresponding decrease in the number of passengers who survive accidents or incidents (Muir & Marrison, 1989). The actions of passengers on flights where there is an incident or accident is a crucial factor in determining the degree to which they are injured and the number of fatalities that occur. This is pertinent given the fact that 90% of passengers survive the initial impact in an accident where death is not inevitable (Muir & Marrison, 1989), and the majority of fatalities occur in the post-impact period. The number of fatalities depends in large measure upon four different variables: (1) the physical features of the aircraft; (2) the level of competence of the crew and rescue services; (3) the environmental conditions both inside and outside the aircraft; and (4) the behaviour of individual passengers and the group.

Passengers' responses to the accident can include one or a number of different behaviours. The most usual of these is fear, particularly pre-impact, and also in the post-impact period where the conditions pose a threat to life. This is commonly accompanied by anxiety associated with and implementing the best strategy to maintain life. These physiological reactions can lead to a variety of behaviours that can either improve or reduce the passenger's chance of survival. Behaviours that interfere with the passengers' ability to effectively manage the post-impact situation include disorientation, depersonalization, panic, behavioural inaction and affiliate behaviour, that of searching out familiar objects or people.

Interaction between the aircrew and passengers can be crucial in guiding passenger behaviour to maximize their opportunities for survival in the event of an accident. As such, cabin crew must inspire the confidence of passengers in respect of their safety. This may have a negative consequence in that passengers may abdicate their own responsibilities to the crew, which may, in turn, lead to behavioural inaction. In addition, during an emergency and after an accident the relationship between cabin crew and passengers changes dramatically. Cabin crew must quickly take charge of passengers to guide them to safety and instantly relinquish their role as flight attendants who provide nicely parcelled trays and headsets for listening to music. This sudden shift in roles can be jarring and confusing for passengers in a state of shock.

The impact of crew behaviour on air safety has been strongest in the flight deck environment. As safety measures on aircraft systems have become progressively more complex, the cause of air accidents has been attributed increasingly to pilot error. Approximately two thirds of all accidents are considered to be caused by pilots, and having resulted from a failure on the flight deck to manage the flight resources appropriately and, on occasion, from the improper use of the controls (Helmreich, 1987). The behaviour of the crew is strongly determined by the "culture" of the flight deck, which is often highly structured and hierarchical (Foushee, 1984). For example, subordinate crew members may be reluctant to challenge the captain about what may be perceived as a questionable decision. The impact of this "culture" may be exacerbated by the fact that a small number of individuals are required to execute a very large number of complex tasks. In this environment, group processes and individual personalities can play a pivotal role in overall performance and safety. Readers may be interested to note that the measures that airlines are now taking as part of flight crew training and subsequent monitoring are being introduced into other technical and highly demanding work situations. These include, among other environments, hospital operating theatres, and are designed to improve communication, reduce error, ameliorate safety, and basically, also, to prevent legal action from being taken against team and their employers (Helmreich, 2000).

Research suggests that some air accidents that are attributed to pilot error result from a breakdown in crew coordination, where crews that make a large number of errors are characterized by a lower level of communication, interaction, and integration. The quality of communication is of particular relevance, and crews that regularly share flight status information, as well as confirm information given, were found to make the fewest errors. Crews that made a large number of performance errors tended, on the other hand, to communicate in ways that were ambiguous, irritable, uncomfortable, or involved a high level of disagreement among crew members (Foushee & Manos, 1981). Flight-crew behaviour has been addressed by airlines through the implementation of Crew Resource Management (CRM) training aimed at developing effective communication procedures and task identification and delegation within small but hierarchically based dyadic or triadic teams on the modern flight deck. Aerospace psychologists have come to play an important role in CRM training, in terms both of facilitating awareness of group dynamics and of looking at individual psychodynamic processes, helping people to understand more about their intrinsic personality structures in specific work situations.

Jet lag

Jet lag (technically called "circadian desynchronization") is now commonly used to describe the disruption that occurs to one's sleeping pattern when travelling on long-haul flights. Air travel can produce a wide range of discomforts that may be physical or psychological in nature, or both. To the seasoned traveller, these discomforts may be a familiar inconvenience, while for the uninitiated they can be an unpleasant surprise. Of all the problems associated with long-distance air travel, jet lag is possibly the most distressing and unwelcome, as it does not disappear on arrival. Indeed, it may take some days to recover from jet lag, and in certain cases it might last for as long as up to two weeks.

The effects of jet lag may prevent the air traveller from enjoying the start of a holiday, getting down to planned business, or adjusting to regular routines upon return home. A change in the times of waking and sleeping cause the traveller's "internal" clock to be unsynchronized with that of the country of arrival (Waterhouse, Reilly, & Atkinson, 1997).

The body uses cycles or internal rhythms that are regulated by the release of hormones and include a hormone to lower its temperature in preparation for sleep. The body temperature starts falling at around midnight, and is at its lowest level at around 4.00 a.m. It then rises again at around 10.00 a.m., and it remains reasonably constant for the rest of the day. Other changes that occur as a result of the body clock are a sudden fall in blood pressure at night and a slowing of breathing and digestive activity.

As jet lag is closely associated with daylight changes as the passenger moves across time zones, the effect is more marked for those travelling in an easterly direction, and for longer journeys. The symptoms can be intense, long-lasting, and cumulative for the frequent traveller. Commonly, air passengers experience extreme fatigue, accompanied by insomnia, loss of appetite, depression, irritability, poor concentration, physical pains and aches, and reduced physical and mental performance. The severity of jet lag is mediated by a number of factors, including the number of time zones crossed, direction of travel, age, gender, as well as frequency of flights.

Strategies to minimize jet lag include efforts to synchronize the traveller's body clock with the time zone of destination country by adjusting their sleeping, eating, and socializing habits. Travellers should be encouraged, wherever possible, to adjust the routines of their life prior to their trip, which may include eating early or going to bed late for a few days before the journey. For journeys where the arrival time is early morning, strategies to induce sleep are especially important, and include creating the right conditions by reducing noise and light, relaxation techniques, and, if necessary, short-term medication. Travellers can also use short naps to gain sleep, but the length of these must depend upon the duration of the visit, to the destination of the country, as naps over four hours in length can "reset" the internal clock to local time. Alternatively, travellers who arrive in the daytime may use different strategies to make themselves more alert, including brief exercise or a high-protein meal to boost energy levels.

Strategies for minimizing general discomfort include wearing appropriate clothing on board aircraft, eating light food, and avoiding caffeinated, alcoholic, or carbonated drinks. The stress associated with physical discomfort is especially relevant on board aircraft in view of restrictions of space and mobility. The added threat of deep-vein thrombosis means that passengers should be encouraged to develop on-board exercise programmes with particular emphasis on stretching techniques, and taking occasional strolls.

Impact of travel on relationships

Stress associated with travel may produce negative consequences socially, psychologically, and physically. However the stress levels experienced will depend upon the individual's prior psychological resiliency. Passengers can improve their capacity to manage stress associated with their journey by adopting a positive, practical, and proactive stance towards the physical, social, and emotional problems that may be encountered.

The negative effects of travel on the non-travelling partner and family members also have a significant impact on the level of stress experienced by the passenger. Air travellers should be encouraged to acquire strategies for managing their relationships with those close to them, particularly with regard to explicit communication regarding the journey and the effect that it may have for all parties. Separations among family members also provide a unique opportunity for speaking about relationships and about what may be viewed as important. Passengers who have been abroad for extended periods may find returning home stressful and as demanding as arriving in any new and unfamiliar environment—a phenomenon referred to as "reverse culture shock". Homesickness can also lead to emotional arousal. This may be characterized by obsessional thoughts about home and negative thoughts about the new environment, and it may be accompanied by low mood. Travellers should acknowledge their nostalgia and develop skills to ensure that they achieve appropriate social support. They should, however, endeavour to create involvement and a degree of commitment with their new environment and also be persuaded to engage in physical activity, all of which can be used to mitigate against the negative feelings associated with homesickness (van Tilburg, Vingerhoets, & van Heck, 1996)

Regular separation from loved ones is a problem that has been termed "the intermittent husband syndrome" (Rigg & Cosgrove, 1994), whereby the partner and family of aircrew exhibit symptoms of increased psychological stress in their daily lives, particularly just preceding going on duty and on their return. Disruption to personal relationships is accepted by many frequent travellers. While travel disrupts attachment patterns in family and social relationships, the extent of the disruption may vary. It has been observed that anxiously attached partners become increasingly more clingy at the point of separation and exhibit intense forms of attachment behaviours—turning around to wave endlessly, touching their partners at the airport gate, and so on. Those individuals who may be deemed more securely attached appear to be content with a simple peck on the cheek and then turn on their heels to board the aircraft (Fraley & Shaver, 1998). Psychologists should recognize that patients with early histories of separation and loss will therefore be potentially more vulnerable to anxious behaviours at the airport, as travellers experience a reactivation of earlier experiences of loss.

Risk-taking behaviour among travellers

Most of what has been described so far deals with passengers on board aircraft. This short section deviates slightly from this context to consider some of the risks to the traveller in a foreign environment, and how these may arise. Public health specialists and behavioural scientists are concerned with disease prevention and treatment compliance. Surveys of travel clinic attendees repeatedly confirm that travellers worry about becoming unwell while abroad, due to eating certain foods or drinking contaminated water. Although the effects of such contamination may be unpleasant, they are rarely life-threatening, and it is possible to reduce the risk of gastrointestinal illness while abroad. Research carried out among returning travellers has demonstrated that unfortunately a significant proportion of travellers fail to take the necessary precautions or heed the advice given by experts and are unnecessarily exposed to other and potentially more serious medical conditions. This also happens in spite of their knowledge and awareness of the risks. Three common examples are (1) contracting malaria by not taking prophylaxis, or not completing the full course of treatment; (2) exposure to sexually transmitted infections, including HIV, through unprotected intercourse with a partner abroad; and (3) sunburn—and the increased risk of skin cancer—after not adequately protecting exposed skin.

Although these are different health problems, the common thread of risk-taking among travellers links them together. There are several possible explanations for travellers taking unnecessary risks:

1. When people are away from home and their usual routine, different decisions may be reached about the acceptability of certain risks; for example, someone may choose to have a brief extramarital affair while on a business trip because he or she believes that it poses no significant threat or risk to their relationship with their regular partner. Similarly, having to take medication to prevent malaria may be equated with ill health, and this belief may conflict with the sense of fun and relaxation normally associated with recreation and with being on holiday. This may be further exacerbated by some of the unpleasant effects of taking malaria prophylaxis. Some travellers may also argue in this case that since they did

not detect any mosquito bites on their body, they could not have contracted malaria, thereby justifying their decision not to take prophylaxis. There are attendant risks to gambling behaviour of this kind.

2. Prevention of some health problems is often associated with having to give up something enjoyable, exposure to something unpleasant, or the inconvenience of having to take measures to prevent exposure to prevent infection or risk. In the case of sexual risk, this may necessitate the use of condoms, while to prevent malaria, a course of medication may need to be completed for the duration of the period of exposure to the infection and for several weeks thereafter. Each of these situations is associated with having to weigh up relative risk and the possibility of inconvenience associated with behavioural change.

3. In terms of sexual risks, some people make judgements about the degree of risk to which they believe they will be exposed on the basis of the physical appearance of their partner or partners. Patient returning from abroad will sometimes say to their health-care professional, "He looked too healthy to be ill or infected", or, "She was too young, and very good-looking, and just didn't seem to be the type." Of course, these beliefs are unreliable because sexual infections can be transmitted irrespective of the age or appearance of the person who may be infected but is free from obvious symptoms. The theory of cognitive dissonance (Festinger, 1957) suggests that we are prone to making up explanations to fit with our beliefs rather than with objective facts. A further example of this strategy to manage dissonance is the smoker who says that the risk to one's health of smoking is manageable because only a small proportion of smokers contract cancer.

Health-care professionals who work with travellers should inform them of the risks and encourage behavioural change where appropriate. Intentions are a reasonable predictor of behaviour. Young, single men travelling abroad with friends are at greatest risk for health problems, for two reasons: first, they may intend to take sexual or other risks while abroad; second, the group may influence the individual or his intentions—for example, to tan responsibly, or to take condoms when planning a night out. Co-factors such as alcohol use may further influence risk-taking behaviour. Counselling of travellers should therefore include some discussion about how they intend to manage different risks across a range of scenarios, including rehearsal of possible situations linking these to both beliefs and actions.

The role of the health-care professional is crucial in informing air travellers about the necessary precautions they should take before their flight to manage the stress associated with their journey. The greatest risk to the traveller's health is non-compliance to the advice given by the health professional. Treatment non-compliance is the most likely outcome where the advice given is incomplete or conflicts with information obtain from other sources. Compliance with advice is also reduced when travellers find the information complex or confusing. It is therefore important to elicit feedback from the individual about how he or she understands the information that is given and to provide an opportunity for questions to be asked.

The aim of this chapter was to provide a psychological understanding of airline passenger behaviour, drawing on published research and clinical material. The more commonly occurring psychological problems experienced airline passengers are also described. Given the unique conditions that air travellers must endure, it should not be surprising that even the most resilient of travellers may experience disruption to their social lives, as well as numerous challenges to their emotional and physical states. Some of the unpleasant effects begin well before actual travel commences and may continue for a period after arriving at one's destination. Most of the issues and psychological problems discussed are by no means confined to the air traveller. It would be wrong to give the impression that air travellers suffer from psychological problems more frequently or intensively than is found in the general population, although the underlying causes, specific triggers, and unique consequences may differ. Nonetheless, some understanding of the interplay between environmental factors and psychological symptoms among air travellers is necessary. Aircrew and passengers share the same environment, and it is reasonable to assume, therefore, that they are exposed to similar stressors. The following chapter explores the unique mental health issues pertaining to aircrew.

CHAPTER THREE

The mental health of pilots

Introduction and history

Thus far, we have explored the psychology of the passenger or air traveller. We now turn our attention to the mind of the airline pilot, and to the role that mental health care professionals may play in understanding the demands of the job, the unusual lifestyle of the pilot, and the stresses that potentially burden the pilot. This review provides an opportunity to assess what is commonly known about mental health issues among pilots, thereby providing an insight into recent research and the types of clinical interventions that may be required. The emphasis is on the medical certification of pilots, psychological problems among aircrew, substance misuse, suicide, psychological reactions to incidents and trauma, and the effects on pilots' personal relationships of their job situation.

Pilots are in many ways a unique occupational group. Their training is both intense and vigorous, and the tasks that pilots perform demand good physical health and psychological stabil-

39

ity. As individuals, they have to be proficient in handling complex systems on board aircraft, as well as have an ability to work as part of a small team or crew. As shift-workers, they do not usually follow the same work routine, and their "office" is normally a cramped flight deck on board a military or commercial aircraft 35,000 feet in the air. Increasing automation on the flight deck over the past decade has altered the role of the modern pilot. While "stick-and-rudder" skills are still important, especially in emergency situations, there is much greater emphasis on managerial tasks, communications, and computer programming. When operating as part of a crew, a pilot's actions are subject to the close monitoring of other crew members, which is likened to an incessant driving test. Regular simulator and line tests, as well as medical assessments for physical and psychological fitness, and a comparatively low retirement age, all add to the stress of the job (Foushee, 1984).

The terrorists' actions in the United States on 11 September 2001 have affected the close-knit pilot community, and it may have adverse and lasting psychological, social, and economic consequences. Not only is there now a greater threat to life aboard aircraft and a real and understandable concern about security, but the economic repercussions for the airline industry worldwide are likely to be far-reaching. It has been estimated that at least 100,000 airline employees will lose their jobs in the years following the terrorists attacks and the ongoing threat of further atrocities. Countless others will be indirectly affected by the abrupt and drastic changes in commercial aviation. Unemployment increases the risk for mental ill health due to the individual's loss of structure, purpose, identity, status, and social contacts, all of which are accompanied by extended periods of inactivity (Winefield, 1995). While many pilots may themselves be resilient in the face of occupational uncertainty, their families, partners, and friends may put increased pressure on some to give up their jobs. After all, a number of flight deck and cabin crew personnel died as a result of these terrorist actions. These are uncertain and turbulent times for pilots.

The popular image of a pilot is someone who is cool, calm, and collected, male, sexy, in control, carrying significant responsibilities, and of someone who enjoys a glamorous life-style. This stereotype is partially upheld within the flying community itself. Much emphasis has been placed on personality types of pilots as people who are deemed to have "the right stuff" in terms of attitudinal variables. Although stereotypes among the flying community do exist, there are variations, including the fact that there are, of course, female aviators! However, the preferred personality traits of pilots include a strong tendency towards being active, self-confident, and competitive, with a tendency towards perfectionism. These are in preference to a pilot exhibiting a lack of conscientiousness, assertiveness, arrogance, impatience, or lacking interpersonal warmth and sensitivity.

Psychologists have made important contributions to aviation from its earliest days, particularly with regard to cognitive psychology, human performance, and limitations, ergonomics, and flight safety (Helmreich, 1987). Less well known is the unique and specific role of the aerospace clinical psychologist whose expertise is in the assessment, treatment, and prevention of psychological problems mainly among aircrew, but also among related personnel, such as air traffic controllers and cabin crew and their families. Those mental health specialists working in this field may be confronted with complex dilemmas and difficult decisions, such as determining whether an individual is fit to become a pilot or to return to flying duties following a psychological problem, ranging from an anxiety disorder to head injury. They also provide consultations about promoting physical and psychological health, such as weight loss and control, stress management, and the dangers of alcohol and substance misuse. Counselling for family and relationship problems, post-incident stress, loss of medical certification, and fear of flying are also part of the remit of clinical and counselling psychologists who work within the airline industry (Senechal & Traweek, 1988).

Aircrew may either be referred by a specialist aviation doctor or line manager, or they may self-refer to a mental health professional. Irrespective of the source of the referral, it has been observed that pilots generally dislike being interviewed by mental health professionals (Jones, Katchen, Patterson, & Rea, 1997), because they do not feel in control of the situation, which goes against their nature. They may feel uncomfortable in a context where they are unfamiliar with the rules and fear the implications of the encounter, which could, after all, jeopardize their flying career and their livelihood if it leads to their licence being revoked. Some may react to the situation by exhibiting overt displeasure, appearing uncooperative, or behaving in a passive–aggressive manner. Others may deny the presence or the severity of their problems or wish to set the record straight about what they perceive to have been a misunderstanding in the referrer's view of the problem. Of course, many are indeed cooperative and welcome the opportunity to discuss their problems.

The apparent reluctance among some pilots to consult with a psychologist is not confined to normal apprehension about unfamiliar situations. It may also be indicative of the fact that psychology is not a precise science and is subject to the personal biases of the interviewer and those charged with evaluating mental fitness. Unfortunately, there are significant challenges to improving our understanding of mental health issues among pilots, because there is a reluctance to approve or fund studies within the industry, owing to concerns about the use to which the information might be put and the possible threat of loss of flying status or legal action if negative findings are reported. In spite of limitations of an understanding of mental health processes among aircrew, it is an undisputed fact that psychological factors influence pilots' performance. A pilot, like any other individual, faces the normal stresses of everyday life. However, the extent to which these problems interfere with flying duties must always be considered and, if appropriate, specialist assessment and treatment must be sought.

It was assumed from the earliest of flying days that those who could ride a horse, literally, would make the best pilots; however, conjecture soon gave way to fact, and more appropriate and reliable selection methods were instigated. The scientific approach to aircrew behaviour and performance was given huge impetus during the First World War, when it became evident that the high accident and fatality rate among pilots was attributable more to pilot error than to enemy action. Further-more, many pilots developed a fear of flying during their train-ing following mishaps from when they returned from combat. The term "aero-neurosis" was first coined by Oliver Gotch, a Royal Navy physician, just 16 years after the Wright brothers first flew, thereby describing an occupational neurosis (Ander-son, 1919). In order to prevent the high attrition rates among students and qualified pilots, methods of pilot selection had to improve, and specialists had to develop ways to assess and treat those with mental health problems.

A special medical board of the Royal Flying Corps was formed in 1916 to deal with the selection of flying officers and to process those deemed unfit to continue with their training or service, including those who had suffered mental breakdowns. In 1917, standards of fitness were drawn up and agreed, and the psychological components for pilots played a significant part in this. It is noteworthy that almost all of those involved in these boards were senior medical and surgical personnel who them-selves had also learned to fly. It was recognized that the routine of the post–World-War-I aviator was characterized by "long spells of idleness punctuated by intense fear" (Anderson, 1919, p. 17)—hence, a very stressful profession. Psychological suitabil-ity was described in terms of "temperament". After visual acu-ity, this temperament was considered one of the most important attributes, though it was acknowledged even at this very early stage in the history of aviation psychology that it was a difficult matter to assess clinically, especially when examining the avia-tor candidate.

It is interesting to note that many of the observations, classi-fications, and recommendations made by Surgeon-Lieutenant H. Graeme Anderson (1919) and Oliver Gotch are still valid today, but with one major exception: there was a greater toler-ance of alcohol use among pilots in those early days in order to subjugate anxiety, though there was recognition that an excess in alcohol use would ultimately ruin the career of the pilot.

The armed forces have been the greatest source with regard to understanding the mental aspects of flying. In spite of the seemingly obvious differences between military and civilian flying concerning levels of risk, flying at unusual angles, and differences in work routine, there are greater similarities between these groups of pilots, and therefore many insights can be applied to both groups.

Psychological requirements
for medical certification

There can be few other professions that require as frequent and rigorous health checks as a condition of certification to work as must be endured by pilots. The risk of losing one's job and livelihood is confronted by professional pilots as often as every six months. The medical standards that have to be met by pilots are laid out by aviation authorities, and are broadly similar throughout the world. The U.S. Federal Aviation Administration (FAA) and European Joint Aviation Regulation (JAR) medical standards stipulate almost identical criteria—with those of the FAA arguably being more clearly defined—and are considered the benchmark for determining pilots' medical fitness. The psychological requirements for medical certification state that pilots must not be suffering from any mental disorders or neurological conditions, or be dependent upon alcohol or recreational drugs. A past history of any of these can also serve as grounds for exclusion (see Reinhart, 1997, for a more thorough list of requirements and exclusions).

A pilot may not act in command of an aircraft or as part of a flight crew if they have a medical or psychological problem that would make them unable to meet the requirements for their current medical certificate. The use of any prescribed or non-prescribed drug that may interfere with a pilot's faculties and threaten safety also invalidates medical certification. A recent history or sudden onset of a medical or psychological problem is therefore covered through certification. In view of the stringent requirements for psychological fitness, a history or diagnosis of the following mental disorders or states automatically leads to initial denial of medical certification and consequently spells the end of any hope of acquiring a pilot's licence:

1. psychosis;
2. affective disorders (including bipolar disorder);
3. personality disorders (especially where there has been evidence of overt acts of violence);
4. substance dependence (alcohol, sedatives, hypnotics, antidepressants, recreational and illicit drugs, and inhalers);
5. substance abuse (within the preceding two years, including positive drug test results, misuse of substances that would interfere with the person's ability to perform the duties of a pilot, or record of drink/drug convictions);
6. neurosis;
7. self-destructive acts;
8. disturbance or loss of consciousness;
9. transient loss of control of nervous system functioning without satisfactory explanation of the cause;
10. epilepsy or convulsive disorders;
11. progressive disease of the nervous system.

Medical and psychological assessment of pilots is by interview, physical examination, and appropriate tests where indicated (Jones & Marsh, 2001). Candidates are also required to complete a questionnaire that authorizes the FAA or JAR to investigate further for drink and alcohol offences and provide examiners with information about visits to psychologists, clinical social workers, or related professionals for substance abuse or psychiatric evaluation or treatment within the preceding three years. This specifically excludes consultations for help with stress, relationships, and other situational problems. The penalties for failing to disclose information or being untruthful include hefty fines and custodial sentences. The pilot's insurances may also be jeopardized as a consequence of falsification. Even if one were to pass an initial medical examination based on there being no evidence of symptoms of either psychological or medical impairment, the onset of a new problem can automatically disqualify an already licensed pilot. Where the pilot feels that an unfair decision has been made over medical certification, there is an appeals procedure, and evidence can be submitted from other sources testifying to the pilot's abilities in an attempt to persuade the licensing authorities to reverse their decision.

Pilots are required to maintain optimum physical and psychological fitness. High levels of responsibility for manoeuvring aircraft, transporting other crew and passengers, coping with demands and decisions, all require mental capability, excellent health, and emotional stability. The purpose of having regular medical assessments in the aviation industry is to preserve the safety of airline passengers, crew, and those on the ground. Aviation authorities and employers have similar aims in this regard. The latter, however, not only wish to maintain safe air transport operations, but also to employ medically fit pilots with a long career ahead, especially in view of the high cost of training pilots (Anthony, 1988).

Pilots operate in unique physical conditions. At times, their work environment can be harsh. They may be exposed to changes of temperature and pressure, high g-forces (gravitational changes), and hypoxia. Even those with perfect vision may sometimes find it difficult adjusting to an array of optical challenges. Needless to say, pilots must be free from a number of specific medical conditions, though this does not imply perfect health.

Psychological problems among aircrew

Psychological problems among aircrew are an insidious threat to aircrew safety because of the impairments to task performance. These may range from minor, transient stress to enduring personality and lifestyle problems, with potentially serious consequences for the individual pilot as well as for passengers. The psychological functioning of pilots becomes especially significant when one realizes that pilots have to deal not only with the unique pressures of flying aircraft, but also the with daily, normal pressures of life (Jones et al., 1997). An understanding of issues pertaining to issues of pilot mental health is timely and warranted for the following reasons:

1. Psychological problems among aircrew may impair performance and therefore compromise safety.

2. There are considerable legal and financial consequences for pilots and their employers following aircraft incidents and accidents, especially where human factors are thought to play a part in these.

3. Selection and training of aircrew carries with it the risk in that it is not possible to predict with complete accuracy which candidates become successful pilots. Psychiatric disturbance among students and qualified pilots in the United Kingdom has been reported to be the most common source of attrition and loss of licence after physical disorders, such as those resulting from cardiovascular disease (Bennett, 1983; Smith, 1983), and, understandably, there is interest in both the airline industry and military in identifying those most at risk for psychological problems as early as possible in their training or career.

4. The job of the modern pilot may itself exacerbate or cause psychological problems: stress, jet lag, fatigue, disrupted personal relationships, unusual routines, frequent medical assessments may all take their toll on even the most resilient crew members.

5. Recent changes in patterns of employment and piloting tasks may be an additional source of stress. This includes a decrease in the proportion of commercial pilots drawn from the military, where previously one would have had access to carefully maintained longitudinal assessment of aircrew. There is an increased mobility among pilots seeking jobs and promotion and a willingness to work abroad. There is greater cultural mix on the flight deck due to pilot mobility and rapid growth in the commercial airline industry. Increased auto-

mation on the flight deck and greater emphasis in the pilot's job on monitoring and managing, rather than on hands-on flying, has meant that many pilots have had to re-learn their role and skills;

6. There is a growing trend towards operating commercial aircraft with a two-person dyadic crew rather than the four- or three-person crews that were more common until the 1980s, with the concomitant change in relationship dynamics and mutual monitoring patterns.

7. There are increased checks and random monitoring, particularly with regard to alcohol and drug use among pilots.

From their initial training to commanding the largest and most sophisticated aircraft, pilots are required to undergo frequent medical and proficiency checks for the duration of their flight career. While reaching the early retirement threshold for pilots is likely to end the career of most, ill health or the loss of their medical certificate will sometimes prematurely or abruptly end the career of others. There are numerous contexts where a pilot's proficiency and mental health are assessed. These include frequent line checks with more senior pilots, simulator checks, and bi-annual health assessments conducted by AME's (Aviation Medical Examiners). In addition, most commercial flights are multi-crew operations, and therefore the actions of each pilot are monitored by their crew partner whenever they fly.

The most commonly presenting psychological problems in aircrew are alcohol abuse, anxiety, marital conflict, somatization, depression, and phobic reactions. Misconduct and antisocial behaviour account for approximately 10% of psychological problems among pilots (Picano & Edwards, 1996). Unfortunately, no up-to-date data have been published on the specific prevalence of different psychological disorders among aircrew, though we know that psychiatric problems are high on the list of medical conditions leading to the loss of licence both in professional aircrew and private pilots in the U.K. (Bennett, 1983). Psychosis and serious personality disorders are rare and inevitably spell the end of the pilot's career, with or without treatment.

Alcohol misuse among pilots is a well-recognized problem and is dealt with in a separate section.

Most of the problems are transient and can be identified via standard psychological and psychiatric treatment methods. By their very nature, however, not all psychological problems are amenable to simple psychological detection. Some may elude discovery altogether, or their onset may come later in the career of a pilot, after many years of problem-free flying. Pre-existent or sub-clinical problems may be noticed only at times of stress that may be difficult to simulate during formal medical assessment. In addition, such problems may be masked by the "halo effect", by assigning greater recognition to the pilot's performance and achievements over their psychological limitations. The choice of career that involves extensive travel might also, for a small number of pilots, be their means to escape from personal problems.

Apart from gross symptoms and obvious signs of mental illness (such as florid psychosis or clinical depression), or behavioural disturbance (due, for example, to alcohol intoxication), it is unreasonable to expect aircrew themselves to be aware of and to be able to detect serious psychological problems in their colleagues. Unfortunately, crew rostering patterns mitigate against the formation of close and enduring working relationships between pilots in which subtle changes in mental health could be readily noticed over a period of time.

Personality disorder

Personality is distinguished from moods and emotional states that are transient. Personality *traits* become a personality *disorder* when they are found to be inflexible, maladaptive, and cause significant impairment in social and occupational functioning (DSM-IV; American Psychiatric Association, 1994). The diagnosis of personality disorder is made when an adult shows long-standing and pervasive impairments in their ability to work and cooperate with others (Cloninger, Svrakic, Bayon, & Prezybeck, 1997). This negative impact on others is crucial to the diagnosis of personality disorder (Tyrer, Casey, & Ferguson, 1993). Thus, personality disorder could have a serious impact on a pilot's functioning and is a clinically indispensable concept. Nonetheless, there are serious obstacles to the accurate detection and assessment of personality disorder. While personality disorder is officially recognized, there is considerable concern with the reliability and validity of the diagnosis in the scientific literature. Indeed, current classification of personality disorder is being seriously challenged by empirical data. It is anticipated that new personality disorder taxonomy will be developed that is more adequately routed in empirical data (see Livesley, 2001). Notwithstanding current shortcomings, personality disorder is highly relevant to assessing pilots' fitness to fly.

Serious personality problems are likely to be detected at an early point in a pilot's career—probably during training—as he/she is likely to "act out", leading to disciplinary problems. However, those with less serious personality disorders are unlikely to be removed at an early stage. These individuals typically lack flexibility and often have interpersonal problems, and these problems may become exacerbated if they are required to assume greater responsibility. In addition, personality disorder often gives rise to or is associated with alcohol problems and emotional disorders such as depression. Individuals with personality disorders often alienate others. Consequently, the pilot with a personality disorder may have difficulty gaining social support during times of stress and may then employ excessive drinking or other "acting-out" coping behaviours.

While emotional disorders such as depression can be diagnosed in a single consultation with a mental health practitioner, multiple sources of evidence are usually required for a reliably personality disorder assessment. Psychological testing can provide useful information in evaluating a pilots personality problems but the accuracy of psychological tests is not sufficient for establishing a diagnosis of personality disorder. In addition, the personality test employed needs to include a measure of defensiveness, as pilot applicants for air carriers are frequently defensive on psychological tests (Butcher, Morfitt, Rouse, & Holden, 1997). Similarly, there is a high likelihood that a pilot is likely to be defensive in a one-off consultation, and additional source of evidence will be needed to establish whether he or she has significant problems.

Disruption to personal relationships

It is the nature of the aviation industry that individuals are removed from their home or environment, often for long periods of time. It would appear from the literature that the role of this life stress in pilots has been insufficiently appreciated by both pilots and researchers alike. However, there is some recognition of the significance and complexity of such stress and its relationship to the function of aircrews and their families. Some studies demonstrate the importance of one's spouse's indirect contribution to flight safety. The conclusions point to more stable marriages predicting better pilot performance (Rigg & Cosgrove, 1994). Given the complex nature of the issue, it is difficult to establish the nature of causality in this respect. It may be that pilots who are happy and in stable relationships perform better in their job. Equally, the satisfaction derived from high levels of competence in one's job might lead to a happier domestic life.

Some researchers point out that where a previously well-functioning and non-anxious pilot suddenly becomes overly concerned about flying duties, family issues should always be addressed (Jones et al., 1997). It has long been recognized that stable spouse and family relationships can act as a buffer against stress in the workplace; conversely, discord in close relationships may intensify stress, leading to impaired work performance. The "spousal factor" in promoting flight safety requires much greater research and understanding (Cooper & Sloan, 1985a, 1985b). Nonetheless, the direct association between stability in spousal relationships and work stress, and ultimately with airline safety, makes this an important issue in pilot training and how pilots cope with and manage the everyday stresses of personal relationships (Karlins, Koh, & McCully, 1989).

In their research on the coping strategies of commercial airline pilots, researchers Cary Cooper and Stephen Sloan discovered that overall mental ill health in pilots has a very strong association with lack of autonomy at work, with fatigue, as well as well the inability to relax, and also the lack of sufficient social support (Cooper & Sloan, 1985a, 1985b; Sloan & Cooper, 1986). Raschmann, Patterson, and Schofield (1990) extended the work on the psychosocial lives of pilots and noted that pilots who suffer from marital distress may be less able to concentrate effectively on their piloting duties and responsibilities. On a more positive note, Karlins, Koh, and McCully (1989) have helped us to appreciate that in an "airline marriage" the spouse can provide extensive social support, thus aiding the pilot in dealing effectively with psychosocial stressors. Disruption to personal relationships is accepted as a reality by many aircrew; the consequences, however, are not sufficiently understood or appreciated.

Contrary to some popular wisdom, flight crew may themselves experience a fear of flying. This may be indicative of a generalized anxiety problem, other personal problems, or a specific performance-related anxiety following an accident. The cumulative pressures of the responsibilities on aviators may also contribute to the prevalence of fear of flying among them. The problem of the fear of flying is often exacerbated by feelings of shame and embarrassment that are likely to delay seeking appropriate treatment (Strongin, 1987).

Pilot reactions to incidents and accidents

Commercial aviation is an ever-growing industry, and accidents, although rare, are unfortunately sometimes catastrophic; when they do occur, public attention is raised, and fear levels and anxieties escalate (Price & Holley, 1990). Whether or not there are fatalities, accidents involving aircraft may have significant and longstanding psychological effects on those directly involved and on the surrounding community (Slagle, Reichman, Rodenhauser, Knoedler, & Davis, 1990). Heightening anxiety in the wake of an airline disaster increases nervousness for all airline passengers and has a ripple effect on crew. Psychological reactions to air accidents have been well documented (Gersons & Carlier, 1993) and cover four main areas. The first concerns those involved with recovery and identification. The second concerns the impact on survivors themselves. The third examines the effects on the surrounding communities in which the accident occurred. To a far lesser extent, the fourth area—and ironically, the most important from a mental health and safety point of view—is for the provision for the debriefing of aircrew, where indicated. While one-off, immediate debriefings are often appreciated by recipients, current recommendations by trauma experts is for a brief psychological intervention in only those individuals whose symptoms do not remit within the expected time frame.

Psychological problems have been found in many survivors of air accidents (Lundin, 1995). PTSD (post-traumatic stress disorder) and depression are the most common psychological outcomes among survivors of the Lockerbie disaster, although a range of other mental health problems were also found (Brooks & McKinley, 1992). It also appears that where PTSD does occur, it may last for a considerable time after the incident. For example, in a study of 175 Royal Air Force officers who survived ejection from their aircraft, 40% experienced prolonged psychological disturbance (Fowlie & Aveline, 1985).

In the case of the Bijlmermeer disaster in Amsterdam in 1992, when an El Al Boeing 747 freighter crashed into two apartment buildings, killing 43 people and making 260 homeless, 26 survivors reported severe PTSD symptoms six months after the crash (Gersons & Carlier, 1993). It has also been found that symptoms of PTSD lasted for up to six months in the case of a hijacking, with a minority of sufferers experiencing high levels of distress (Thompson, 1991). Only one exploratory study could be found that directly addressed psychological reactions among flight crew to an accident. The results suggested that commercial pilots suffer more stress than was previously thought in the aftermath of a major incident, and that the need for post-incident or post-accident counselling needs to be better appreciated and managed. Preventative measures need to be put into place as soon as possible after the accident in order to prevent long-standing psychological consequences (Johnston & Kelly, 1988).

One must, of course, not underestimate the impact of an air disaster on members of the public who witness the crash. Symptoms of PTSD have been found in many of the people who have been indirectly affected by crashes, such as that which occurred near Coventry (Chung, Easthope, Chung, & Clark-Carter, 1999a; 1999; Chung, Easthope, Eaton, & McHugh, 1999). Children's thinking following the space shuttle Challenger disaster in 1986 demonstrated that a whole generation could be affected emotionally by such an event, with symptoms of psychic trauma emerging (Terr, Bloch, Michel, Hong Shi, Reinhardt, & Metayer, 1997). Traumatic responses can be triggered vicariously. It is likely to be no different in the wake of the New York World Trade Center tragedy, in view of the power of the imagery conveyed. We have anecdotal clinical evidence that already suggests that people who had observed the trauma on television have started experiencing a range of anxiety-related symptoms.

Alcohol and drug misuse

Foremost among psychological problems that present among pilots is alcohol misuse. The effects are primarily on the central nervous system and lead to impairment of reaction time, reasoning, balance and coordination, and speech, and to the long-term effects of dementia, impaired memory, rigidity of thought, and problems in relationships, both socially and with colleagues. Epilepsy can also be associated with alcohol dependency, particularly during the early stages. Absenteeism may be the first obvious signal to colleagues at work and in management that there may be a serious problem. Those who suffer from alcohol dependence are more likely to be involved in accidents generally—drink-driving accidents in particular. Alcohol misuse may also be a co-factor in other psychiatric disorders, including anxiety, panic disorder, and depression; and the onset may coincide with bereavement, loneliness, or the break-up of a relationship. It is important therefore to make a full assessment of the personal, social, medical, and occupational circumstances of the pilot who presents with an alcohol problem. This may not always be a simple and straightforward task, as denial of the problem is common, in spite of obvious signs, such as smelling of alcohol, unkempt appearance, shaky hands in the morning, and even a prior drink-driving conviction. Urine analysis, and the more reliable method of hair analysis, are used in the workplace to screen for alcohol and drug misuse.

While alcohol dependency automatically denies pilots medical certification, it is not always possible to exclude even moderate to severe drinkers from piloting aircraft. This is because the problem may go undetected, certain levels of alcohol use are tolerated among pilots, and the dependency may only develop later in the pilot's successful career (Harris, 2002).

The lack of research into alcohol and drug use among pilots until the early 1960s might be explained by the fact that the very thought of pilots flying under the influence of alcohol was a taboo subject. However, it seems that research into ways of combating drug and alcohol use had to be undertaken when it became known that alcohol had an influence in nearly one third of all aviation accidents (Holdener, 1983). A great deal of attention was subsequently paid to alcohol use among pilots, although similar emphasis was not placed upon the continuing importance of research in this particular field. Hence, the effectiveness of such policies has been the subject of very little systematic information (Cook, 1997a). Since in recent years few aircraft incidents have been directly attributable to alcohol use among pilots, the impression given is that there is a degree of complacency regarding research that links alcohol misuse to aircrew behaviour and air safety, in spite of the fact that pilots experience high levels of stress in their jobs and have to endure considerable disruption to their personal lives. Intermittent absences from family and social support, periods of time relaxing and recuperating, sometimes accompanied by boredom and social pressure to consume alcohol with fellow crew members, may be the root cause of alcohol misuse and dependency (Flynn, Sturges, Swarsen, & Kohn, 1993). This is especially the case among general aviation pilots in the United States (Modell & Mountz, 1990).

Alcohol impairs pilot performance even 48 hours after its consumption. It has been claimed that the eight-hour waiting period from "bottle to throttle" used as a standard in several airlines is potentially insufficient (Cook, 1997a, 1997b). There are two main issues that emerge from research into the effects of alcohol upon aircrew performance: even where there appears to be a low blood alcohol concentration (BAC), performance of pilots can still be adversely affected, and due to the negative effects of alcohol after consumption, often characterized as post-alcohol impairment (PAI), aircrew should not fly until their BAC has returned to zero and has stayed at zero for some time. It has been observed that most pilots understand the importance of the first point but underestimate the consequences of the second (Cook, 1997a).

Strategies for the prevention of alcohol misuse among aircrew need to be focused and relevant to the unique and specific demands of piloting and the social and work context of aircrew. Such policies must operate within two given contexts, either by directly specifying how much and when alcohol may be consumed, and by identifying through a screening system who should not fly and then preventing them from doing so (Cook, 1997a, 1997b). While this dual strategy is central to reducing the risk of alcohol-related incidents and accidents, research has demonstrated that it is a struggle to get this message across to pilots. Indirect prevention of alcohol misuse is recommended by the introduction of random alcohol tests prior to flying, general screening, and educating pilots about the dangers inherent in what they may perceive may be normal behaviours relating to alcohol consumption (Cook, 1997a, 1997b). Further measures include prevention of relapse among those treated for dependence and providing support for susceptible individuals (Flynn, Sturges, Swarsen, & Kohn, 1993).

It is well known that certain medications, even those that may seem innocuous, can interfere with a pilot's performance. This is addressed at an early stage in a pilot's training, usually in the context of the so-called "human factors" course, which examines those factors that facilitate or impede the pilot's performance. Surprisingly little has been published on the effects of recreational drug use and their links to performance. It is reasonable to conclude that, similar to alcohol misuse, pilots might underestimate the enduring effects of recreational drug use on their psychological state and motor performance. Airline policies focus predominantly on prevention of alcohol consumption, thus neglecting sufficient attention to the problem of drugs.

Pilot suicide by aircraft

Ultimately, any research into the mental health of pilots should be for the welfare of the pilots themselves, and consequently also for the people that they carry with them on board the aircraft. The need for improved psychological screening of pilots has been called for following a few aircraft crashes in the last decade where the evidence points to pilot suicide being the cause. While the majority of those few pilots who choose to end their lives do so "on the ground" and use methods of suicide reported among victims in the general population, cases of alleged pilot suicide in commercial airline operations are generally considered to be rare, though the absence of specific data makes the true extent difficult to determine. The consequences legally and financially may be far-reaching, since the deliberate crashing of an aircraft as a means of committing suicide may also become a homicide if other crew, passengers, and people on the ground are injured or killed. It has been estimated that between 0.72 and 2.4% of general aviation accidents are as a result of pilot suicide and a history of psychiatric or domestic problems have been found in the post-crash enquiries and investigations (Cullen, 1998).

The National Transportation Safety Board (NTSB) is currently investigating whether suicide was the likely cause of the Egypt Air Flight 990 crash off New York in 1999. Pilot sabotage was suspected in the Silk Air 737 crash in December 1997 where the aircraft plummeted into a river into Indonesia, killing all 104 passengers and crew. Investigators believe that the pilot deliberately flew the plane into the ground. The former military pilot in command had a history of gambling and financial problems and had taken out a life insurance policy the day before the flight. The cause of the crash of a Royal Air Maroc commuter plane in 1994, which killed 54 people, was deemed a case of pilot suicide. In 1982, a Japan Airlines pilot was institutionalized after trying to crash the DC-8 that he was flying into Tokyo's Haneda Airport, killing 24 passengers in the process. In 1998, an Air Botswana pilot informed air traffic control of his intention to fly his empty plane into the president's residence. When deterred, he chose instead to crash it into the remainder of the airline's fleet at the airport at Gabarone. The pilot, believed to have been grounded after an AIDS diagnosis, died in the crash. Miraculously, no one on the ground was injured.

One can only speculate as to the possible reasons why a pilot should want to end his or her life in this way. The desire to protect one's family and memory from shame might be bound up in the belief that any evidence of what happened would be destroyed in the ensuing crash. In some cases, the suicide crash could also be an expression of intense anger towards or revenge for problems that have their origins in the workplace, or a grudge against an employer. Failure to achieve promotion, or even a demotion, might be realistic triggers. Personal problems stemming from debt, relationship difficulties, substance misuse, and mood disorder are, however, more likely causes. When trying to determine whether a pilot's actions—including suicide—were the cause of an accident, events and parameters of different aircraft systems (as recorded on the flight data recorder) and communication on the flight deck (as recorded on the cockpit voice recorder) are replicated in a laboratory or flight simulator. A post-crash "psychological autopsy" where the pilot's life and lifestyle are thoroughly investigated is carried out in order to gain a clearer understanding of suicidal intent prior to the event (Jones et al., 1997). Sadly, denial, feelings of shame, and fear of disclosure may prevent some pilots who are depressed and suicidal from grounding themselves. They may interpret psychological problems as being indicative of failure to demonstrate that they have "the right stuff". They may erroneously believe that having a psychological problem makes them a bad pilot.

Any pilot who exhibits serious psychological problems should be temporarily or permanently grounded. As behaviour prior to a suicide may radically change (e.g. poor motivation and low mood), this makes the need for awareness of mental health issues even more important, especially among fellow aircrew. When assessing the mental health of pilots, it is important to look for predisposing factors that might increase the risk of suicide, and these include alcohol misuse as well as a previous history of psychiatric problems. Although pilots can be trained to look out for signs of mental illness in their colleagues, they may not necessarily be skilled in identifying the signs of depression when these are either concealed or sub-clinical. The prognosis for some aviators in the military who present to mental health specialists expressing suicidal thoughts is generally more favourable if treatment is undertaken and follow-up provided. A number of these pilots subsequently return to full flying duties (Patterson, Jones, Marsh, & Drummund, 2001).

Environmental challenges

Jet lag among aircrew is exacerbated by shift work and long hours of duty. This can lead to pilots becoming more tired, and it may impair their focus and attention, thereby increasing the risk of errors (Caldwell, 1997). Recent research has demonstrated that chronic jet lag in flight attendants can actually lead to temporal lobe atrophy and spatial cognitive deficits over a long period of time (Cho, 2001). After a period of rest, the atrophy associated with repeated jet lag has been shown to diminish, although we do not yet understand the full long-term implications.

Pilot fatigue may have its roots in how duty rosters become organized (Price & Holley, 1990). The combination of duty rosters together with poor nutrition can lead to cognitive errors, and therefore there is a need for vigilance regarding the hours worked (Helmreich, 2000). There seems to be no specific cure as such for overcoming fatigue; however, some recommended measures include paying attention to crew scheduling, enforcement of regulations concerning hours flown, diet adaptation, relaxation techniques, prophylactic napping, and education (Caldwell, 1997).

It is generally assumed that airsickness is not a problem that affects pilots. This is not altogether true. While it is more likely to affect student pilots at the beginning of their training, it can also be a problem for more experienced pilots or aircrew later in their career. There are several causes of airsickness, including sympathetic nervous system over-arousal, conflicting information, anxiety regarding performance, and low mood and apprehension. Generally, the prognosis for pilots who suffer from airsickness is thought to be good, given the aviator's strong motivation to fly. In one study, 35 out of 37 students pilots suffering from recurrent airsickness were able to return to their flight training programme after an airsickness management programme that incorporated cognitive techniques (Giles & Lochridge, 1985). In some cases, however, it may be indicative of a fear of flying or a lapse in motivation, and for this reason it should always be thoroughly investigated. Heat in the confines of a small flight deck, coupled with the "bank angle" or "attitude" (i.e. tilt) of the plane, also causes airsickness.

Responding to the threat of terrorism

One of the most worrying challenges posed to the modern airline pilot is the threat of terrorist actions (hijacking, exploding a bomb, assaulting or executing crew and/or passengers, or commandeering and then deliberately crashing an aircraft into a building or other strategic or symbolic location). Increased security and safety checks, passenger profiling, as well as the advent of the hermetically sealed flight-deck door are but two of the more obvious responses to this threat, though others are also in place. For pilots, the threat heralds the start of a profoundly different relationship with passengers, any of who might be considered a potential terrorist. In the 1970s, when hijackers took command of aircraft as a means to extort or coerce regime change, money, or to free prisoners, one aim was for them to survive the experience. In the modern era, terrorists on board aircraft might think nothing of killing their hostages and taking their own lives in the process, not to mention killing people on the ground.

The response to this new and more deadly threat among pilots has been varied. In the United States, for example, there is strong support among the fraternity for arming pilots either with stun guns or revolvers. The deployment of armed air marshals on board aircraft is almost inevitable on some carriers and on certain routes. While the training of pilots and crew to respond to the threat of terrorist actions on board is well-established practice at El Al, the Israeli national carrier, as is fitting civilian aircraft with anti-missile devices, these precautions are now being seriously considered by many other airlines.

The main implications of the above are two-fold: (a) passenger-crew relationships are potentially more adversarial than at any time in the past, and there is likely to be a concomitant increase in stress and fear among all who travel on board aircraft; and (b) airline crew will increasingly be required to undergo training in handling terrorist threats and in disarming, disabling, or even killing any passenger who threatens the safety of all on board. The latter raises questions about selection and suitability of crew for this purpose. The deployment of air marshals, in response to the former, could go some way to allaying the fears of some who travel, while others may consider this evidence that security on the ground may be failing, and the outcome may be that they become even more cautious or frightened travellers.

Concluding comments

The role of mental health professionals working closely with aeromedical professionals and flight surgeons has been highlighted both in the rigorous pre-selection and testing of aircrew and during the ongoing monitoring of career pilots. It has been suggested that one of the most important purposes of aerospace clinical psychology has been to gain a thorough understanding of just how pilots adapt to and cope with the demands of the job under different conditions and to understand why and how adaptation to this task sometimes fails (Picano & Edwards, 1996).

Although it is unlikely that there will ever be a foolproof method for identifying pilots at greatest risk of psychological problems and those currently suffering from specific disorders, it is nonetheless prudent for mental health care workers, pilots, and employers to keep abreast of current research issues and findings. People's life circumstances and mental state can change, and pilots are no exception. There is no specific evidence that more stringent or robust selection procedures would prevent psychologically vulnerable individuals from becoming pilots. It is important to ensure that pilots have direct and easy access to confidential mental health professionals whom they can consult without fear of adverse repercussions for doing so. It is also important to put mental health provision in a positive, preventative light rather than being regarded as a punitive, threatening measure. As part of their training and ongoing education, pilots should be taught about the basics of common mental health problems, the effects of psychological distress, and ways to improve their ability to identify the more obvious signs in themselves and in colleagues. Scenarios that include pilot incapacitation on the flight deck due to a mental health problem could be included among a range of simulator training exercises. Equally important is to explain what can and should be done to seek professional help at an early stage with the minimum of fuss and stigma. The mystique commonly associated with psychological treatment should also be removed. Airline company policies and the attitude of the regulatory aviation medical authorities are important in helping to achieve these important goals.

Although much is understood about mental health aspects of piloting, there are considerable gaps in the literature, probably with the exception of alcohol misuse. The majority of studies are cross-sectional rather than longitudinal. A range of methodologies is used, with quite a number of case studies being reported in preference to more systematic and longitudinal research based on larger samples. There is also more research carried out among military aviators rather than among civilian pilots. While there are many similarities, there are also some differences, particularly with regard to lifestyle, employment patterns, and the demands of the respective tasks. This might have implications for the generalizability of some of the published findings.

Little is known about the extent to which piloting causes (or mitigates against) psychological problems, or whether different rostering arrangements, where strong attachments could facilitate better working relationships, could improve the dynamics of flight crews and help in the early detection of psychological problems. Most published research focuses on active pilots, and there is surprisingly little on the psychological problems of grounded or retired pilots. Specific data on the prevalence of certain psychiatric problems and syndromes and referral patterns to mental health workers are either unavailable or not closely monitored. This gap may, in turn, adversely affect the quality of available research and the provision of specialist treatment services in this field. We do not know whether the hermetically sealed flight-deck door triggers greater anxiety in passengers and crew, who may consequently feel more remote or detached from one another.

There does not appear to be any evidence from the published literature that greater regulation of pilots would improve or alleviate psychological problems among them. However, certain airline companies and insurers have expressed concerns about the repercussions of incidents and accidents that can be traced back to problems with pilot mental health. The antidote to this anxiety is arguably to increase the understanding of psychological problems among aircrew, to provide better psychological care, and to do so in a spirit of collaboration with pilots. Other professional groups, such as medical doctors, have taken steps to acknowledge and to deal with psychological problems among members of that group. These measures go some way towards reducing the antipathy that is sometimes shown towards mental health professionals.

As mental health professionals, we can make a meaningful, positive, and effective contribution to clinical aerospace psychology; however, there are numerous examples within the field of psychotherapy of the failure of mental health specialists to appreciate the unique and specific problems of certain occupational groups. It is incumbent upon mental health professionals to learn about the demands and experiences of being an aviator if we are to avoid making assumptions about these, thus running the risk of being imperialistic and prescriptive in our treatment methods. Regrettably, mental health professionals play all too minor a role in ongoing assessment and evaluation, which remain predominantly the responsibility of medical examiner, who may or may not be sufficiently psychologically skilled. It is to be hoped that as the field of clinical aerospace psychology develops further, there will be a greater collaboration between aviation medical examiners, flight surgeons, and mental health clinicians.

CHAPTER FOUR

The psychodynamics of travel phobia: a contribution to clinical aerospace psychology

Brett Kahr

There can be few experiences more terrifying than flying in an aeroplane at 35,000 feet through extreme turbulence. As the plane shakes at an almost unthinkable altitude, passengers must sit patiently and probably helplessly, hoping that the tumult will soon disappear. Flying can be a chilling experience, not only because of the potential dangers of being suspended in mid-air, but also in view of the new threats to human safety that have become all too palpable in the wake of the terrorist attacks of 11 September 2001.

Death from flying occurs very infrequently indeed; but in view of the possibility that the aircraft might malfunction through either human error or mechanical error, and in view of the possibility of terrorist hijacking, it would be odd for contemporary passengers not to experience a certain amount of anxiety at the prospect of flying. In my clinical work as a psychotherapist, I have paid a great deal of attention to patients' references to aeroplanes, as they discuss their recent or forthcoming travels. I have noticed that patients' comments about air travel and the prospect of air travel tend to fall into one of three distinct categories:

1.   no detectable anxiety whatsoever;
2.   normal anxiety;
3.   crippling anxiety of phobic proportions.

I must confess that I remain somewhat concerned about those patients who claim to experience no detectable anxiety whatsoever about air travel. In my experience, these individuals may not necessarily be mentally healthy people free from all anxieties; rather, they may represent a cluster of individuals who manage to utilize manic defences and mechanisms of denial not only in their relation to air travel, but in other areas of life as well. One of my patients, a very hard-working businessman who travels extensively, has often joked: "Listen, if I die in an explosion, well, then that's it. I won't know about it, and then there'll be nothing to worry about—so why sweat!" Although he claims to be both fearless and cheerful at the prospect of travel, his comments contain very evident traces of the denial of the realistic possibility of death.

By contrast, those patients who report a reasonable amount of anxiety tend to be the healthiest. One of my patients, herself a mental health professional who has had much personal psychotherapy and psychoanalysis over the years, will always telephone her children before a flight, and she will tell them how much she loves them. This colleague knows that from a statistical point of view, the likelihood of dying at 35,000 feet remains very small indeed. An actuary will tell us that one would be more likely to die from being kicked in the head by a donkey than from an air crash! Nevertheless, my patient knows that death can never be avoided, and that flying in an artificially constructed tube at a considerable height will increase one's risk of death; therefore, making contact with her loved ones represents a realistic wish to leave her children with a final affirmation of her love and affection, just in case she should encounter tragedy while airborne.

The third category of patients—namely, those whose anxiety about travel, even before this era of terrorism, could best be described as phobic in nature—represents a much greater challenge to clinicians. These individuals resist travelling at every opportunity, and I have had many patients who have turned down lucrative job opportunities, lecture invitations, or family reunions in order to avoid stepping onto an aeroplane. When these phobic individuals do have to fly, they experience extreme, persistent agitation for days, or even weeks, before departure, and they sleep fitfully the night before their projected flight, often dosing themselves with tranquillizers prescribed by their general medical practitioner. Such individuals frequently report the fantasy of being knocked unconscious before their departure, so that they may magically awaken at their destination without having to have any conscious experience of the flight.

A young child who comes to see me with his parents and siblings for family therapy recently told me about his Christmas trip to the Bahamas. According to this boy, who is eight years of age: "The flight was awesome! We got to watch movies the whole time, and the stewardess took us to see the captain in the cockpit. It was wicked!" This child seemed to show no trace of anxiety at all. Why, then, do so many of our patients experience such distress at the prospect of flying when an eight-year-old boy can manage to experience so much pleasure from the journey?

In view of the virtual ubiquitousness of airline travel, it seems extraordinary that psychoanalysts and psychotherapists have written almost nothing about the subject. And yet, it seems that the very nature of the aeroplane situation cries out for a psychodynamic analysis. As one studies the various components of a journey by air in greater detail, one realizes that the sources of anxiety—even phobic anxiety—make a great deal of sense. To begin with, one must consider the reason for the journey—itself a source of fear or trepidation. Many patients will fear arrival at their destination, which might involve a challenging work opportunity or meeting a relation towards whom one harbours ambivalent affects. And every journey involves separation and uprootedness—one not only travels towards somewhere unknown, but in doing so one leaves behind loved ones, as well as one's more secure foundations of familiarity. By leaving the family home and by leaving "Mother Earth" or "terra firma", literally, allowing oneself to be propelled into the stratosphere, one will invariably experience separation anxiety. Such separation anxiety will be felt more acutely and more pathologically, especially if one has had complex separation experiences during early infancy and childhood. The aeroplane situation can readily reactivate historical scenarios, evoking more primitive terrors. Indeed, recent research has revealed that those individuals who have experienced early episodes of greater separation will become more frightened at the prospect of air travel. In a pioneering study, researchers R. Chris Fraley and Phillip R. Shaver (1998) of the Department of Psychology at the University of California at Davis undertook a naturalistic observational study of couples bidding one another goodbye at a metropolitan airport. On the basis of direct observation and rating scale measures, Fraley and Shaver discovered, unsurprisingly, that those members of the couple with more anxious attachment styles experienced greater distress at the prospect of separation from their partners than did those individuals with more secure backgrounds.

The anxiety of air travel stems not only from the experience of separation from secure objects, or from the anticipatory anxiety of meeting new objects or feared objects, but from other sources as well. Of great importance, one must consider the nature of the relationship between the passengers and the crew on board the aircraft. While buckled into our seats, we remain the relatively passive recipients of caretaking from the flight attendants who serve our drinks and meals, and from the pilot and co-pilot who actually fly the plane. On the whole, most of the flight attendants will be young females, and most of the pilots will be male. Therefore, at an unconscious level, I suspect that we might regard the flight attendants as maternal substitutes, taking responsibility for food and drink, and in constant view. The male pilots, paternal substitutes, will rarely be seen, thus mirroring most grown-ups' experience of early caretakers, which, until recently, involved a relatively present mother who fed us and a relatively absent father who went out to work in order to support the family. Thus, the very structure of the staffing aboard the aeroplane might well replicate the early experience of our childhood homes.

Furthermore, the Mummy and Daddy figures conspire to control the timing of our food and drink and the timing of our use of the lavatories. We may not be served food and drink at particular times (for example, during take-off and landing), and we may not use the toilets at particular times (especially during turbulence, when we must sit with our seatbelts securely fastened). And not only must we wait for the flight attendants to serve our food, but we must deal with our potential rivalrousness towards the other passenger-siblings aboard the plane, many of whom will be served before we receive our plastic tray of food. Thus, as passengers on board an aeroplane, we do not have complete control over our basic alimentary–incorporative or defecatory–expulsive capacities. This situation will undoubtedly encourage regressive behaviours or fantasies: hence the preponderance of air rage, but more especially, the experiencing of fear and terror. As we sit passively strapped into our seats, we do succumb to a certain regressive pull, potentiated by the fact that we sit helpless at 35,000 feet, cared for by parental figures of unknown capabilities.

Not only do we allow ourselves to submit to the authority of the cabin crew and the pilots—we really have no alternative—but, furthermore, we do so at an extraordinary altitude. In my experience, being told that the plane has reached a "comfortable cruising altitude of 38,000 feet" will perhaps reactivate the ordinary infantile anxieties of falling. We know from the most basic developmental psychology experiments in depth perception that very young infants will become trepidatious as they peer over a precipice (cf. Walk, 1979); and we know from the theorization of the paediatrician and psychoanalyst Dr. Donald Winnicott (1967, 1968), in particular, that the fear of falling represents one of the most common anxieties of early infancy. No doubt, these terrors will be reactivated as we cruise on aeroplanes at great heights.

We can readily understand that the very nature of airline travel will not only become a lightning rod for realistic fears and for reasonable fears of crashing or of being caught in a terrorist attack, but that, additionally, our more primitive agonies will become inflamed as air travel forces us to deal with separation and loss, fears of falling, and the regressive situation of having parental substitutes controlling some of our bodily functions amid a gaggle of needy siblings. No wonder so many of us experience fear and loathing at the prospect of travelling on a commercial airliner, quite apart from the medical dangers of deep-vein thrombosis or viral infections.

Hopefully, a conscious knowledge of our increased vulnerability in these circumstances will contribute to an alleviation of our fears and terrors; and hopefully, airline staff will become increasingly aware of the important transferential role that they may serve in the minds of frightened passengers. Just as the psychoanalyst sits out of sight, comforting patients with his or her voice, making sage interpretations, so too must pilots come to realize that their voice over the intercom serves an important transitional function, and that during periods of turbulence the voice of the pilot, offering adult reassurance, can be critical. If pilots do not talk passengers through turbulence, the passengers will more readily develop a fantasy of abandonment, thereby increasing infantile anxiety in unhelpful ways.

It is to be hoped that developments in the interface between modern psychology and modern technology will lead the way in helping individuals to understand the origins of travel phobia more fully, so that airline travel need not be such a source of crippling anxiety.

CHAPTER FIVE

Clinical aerospace psychology in the future: a dialogue

Robert Bor in conversation with Brett Kahr

When reflecting on the contents of this book, we felt that many questions remained unanswered about clinical aerospace psychology and mental health issues among passengers and aircrew. The conversations that ensued between us helped to deepen our understanding of some issues and address certain controversies. They also focused our thinking about the provision of mental health care in this field. We hope that readers might enjoy a departure from regular text and "join" some of the discussion we have had on this interesting topic.

BRETT KAHR: Robert, can you speak about how you became involved in aviation psychology?

ROBERT BOR: As a clinical psychologist and family psychotherapist, I have had a long-standing interest in the ways in which individuals manage journeys throughout the life cycle—both external journeys from country to country and internal journeys from stagnation to growth. On a more concrete level, I have also had an ongoing interest in the realities of air travel itself, and during an earlier period in my life I had even contemplated becoming a professional airline pilot. At British Airways, one particular pilot invited me to visit Cranebank, the British Airways training centre at Heathrow Airport. I spent two hours in the flight simulator, and apparently I had performed sufficiently well that the pilot who had invited me to explore the simulator actually wondered whether in fact I had already acquired a pilot's licence! This encouragement prompted me to pursue formal training for what has been an ongoing personal passion, and I obtained my pilot's licence in 1996. My growing interest in the field of clinical aerospace psychology stems from the blending of my clinical training, my lifelong passion for travel, and my experience as a pilot.

My formal work as an clinical aerospace psychologist began in the mid-1990s, when I had been invited to develop a counselling service for the flight crew of several international airlines. In this context, I began to become more familiar with the internal world of pilots, and I learned a great deal about their lifestyles, their relationships, and the unique problems that they had to face in their "office at 35,000 feet", for the pilots do indeed refer to the flight deck as "the office".

In the wake of events of 11 September 2001, we subsequently learned that some of the terrorists who flew the planes into the World Trade Center and the Pentagon had attended flight schools. Some people have become concerned about how qualified pilots are trained, whether they undergo selection for the training, and whether anyone can simply walk onto an aeroplane and start flying a plane. Readers will be relieved to know that the training of the qualified pilot is actually a rigorous procedure, and that pilots must submit themselves to continued monitoring in order to ensure that their flying licences remain current. Indeed, almost every time a qualified pilot begins to fly a commercial aeroplane, he or she will have at least one other pilot colleague on the flight deck who will be constantly monitoring the pilot's performance every leg of the journey. Physical and mental health checks are part of the on-going licensing requirements for all pilots.

After having undertaken work as a counsellor to pilots and then subsequently having obtained my pilot's licence, I began to work as a therapist to pilots and crew and to their spouses or other family members, who asked for help with conflicts and disruptions in their personal lives. Subsequently, I have counselled individuals who have had to work with airline employees who have themselves had to support the families of employees involved in incidents, and on rare occasions, disasters. Many of these airline workers found themselves suffering from some of the highly recognizable symptoms of post-traumatic stress disorder, especially secondary traumatization, in the wake of working with the survivors and bereaved relatives of those affected by airline accidents.

I also began to work with passengers who have suffered from mild, moderate, or extreme varieties of travel phobia or fear of flying. Although most of the work in treating fearful fliers has been of a brief nature, I have found that it has been necessary to explore clients' life histories in greater detail, and here my training in family therapy has been indispensable. People who present at travel phobia clinics generally baulk at the idea of being referred for a lengthy Freudian psychoanalysis. Therefore, one must find a way of intervening in a reasonably short space of time but also move beyond the traditional cognitive–behavioural modes of treating the symptom and explore the deeper family and systemic issues that may have contributed to the development and maintenance of a travel phobia. Some of this clinical work was developed at the Royal Free Hospital Travel Health Clinic in London.

In the mid-1990s, while I was serving as Professor of Psychology at City University in London, the head of the university's School of Engineering invited me to participate in their newly developed M.Sc. degree programme in Air Transport Management, the equivalent of an M.B.A. for pilots and senior managers in the airline industry. I became involved in teaching the psychology components of that course as well as those on the Diploma in Travel Medicine at the Royal Free Hospital. These experiences also provided the initial stimulus for research in clinical aerospace psychology, both as a supervisor of student research projects, and for my own programme of clinical research. I have looked at unruly passenger behaviour or "air rage", which had become a more widely reported phenomenon. This lead to a research project for the International Civil Aviation Organization (ICAO). My colleagues and I surveyed the world's leading airlines, and we examined both their understanding of the problem and their procedures for dealing with air rage. We have also surveyed the experiences of cabin crew with regard to air rage incidents. We have now turned to examining the recorded incidents of air rage. With the cooperation of senior police colleagues we are examining the histories of the perpetrators of air rage, enquiring whether these individuals "acted out" only on the aeroplane, or whether they had also previously had other chargeable offences while on the ground. It would appear that in some cases, perpetrators have a history of conduct disorder or antisocial personality patterns dating back to their childhood and adolescence. My current research focuses on different aspects of passenger behaviour and the mental health of aircrew.

BK: Robert, can we think about clinical aerospace psychology as a discipline? It seems there are a small number of mental health professionals in the world who are working in this field, or what we are now calling "clinical aerospace psychology". Do you think that this is a field that has potential for growth? Is this is an area that we should be encouraging more mental health practitioners to become involved in? Maybe each airline should have one psychologist on staff to deal with the few cases of intractable fear of flying. What are your thoughts?

RB: I think a large part of mental health practice, particularly in the latter part of the twentieth century, but obviously at the start of the twenty-first century, has been to psychologize different areas of professional practice, ranging from within the legal profession, to medicine, to what we are talking about here, which is the application of psychological ideas and interventions to aerospace. I think the aerospace field is ripe for participation and intervention. I am not sure that we are yet in a position to talk about a whole sub-speciality of clinical aerospace psychology. But it is certainly an area in which mental health practitioners can become more involved.

A question that comes to mind is whether one needs specialized aerospace psychologists, psychiatrists, psychotherapists, counsellors, or clinical social workers who can work in this particular field. We certainly need specialists who will advance research practice and collaborate with pilots, with people within the airline industry, and those people are obviously going to need more specialist knowledge and give more time and develop good working relationships within that particular field. There are also the interests and problems of passengers, a group who are more likely to seek specialist help, particularly with overcoming a fear of flying.

It would be wrong to suggest that there is extensive psychopathology in the aerospace industry, particularly among pilots, air traffic controllers, maintenance personnel, airport managers and so on. . . . I don't think that that is at all the case, and there is no hard evidence to suggest that. I think that there are two areas in which mental health practitioners can play a particular role. One is in preventative mental health work, and that is—as we have seen from the research summarized in this book—a fairly wide range of standard psychological problems that may present, either with passengers or airline employees. Many of these are normal, everyday problems that one would expect to see in most other organizational settings. However, because of the apparent stigma attached to consulting mental health practitioners, some may avoid or delay seeking support. Small problems may intensify and either never be treated or become deeper. The second is in those areas where specific interventions can be introduced. The two areas that I would most have in mind would be to do with assisting qualified medical examiners who assess pilots for their physical and psychological health. That could be in one of two ways: either in direct interventions with the pilots or by offering training to the doctors so as to acquire advanced skills in their mental health assessments. There is another area, and that is to consult to airlines and offer training in mental health issues in aerospace. There are so many areas of interest and relevance, including shift-work patterns, coping with fatigue, managing stress, dealing with angry passengers, and team-work, to name but a few. I was wondering what your views would be about this?

BK: Well, I think that it might be helpful and enlightening for us to try to create an imaginary job description for what the first specialist clinical aerospace psychologist might look like. You made a crucial differentiation between two types of interventions: one dealing with pilots or passengers who have overt mental health difficulties already, and the other in prophylactic or preventative work, to see whether mental health professionals can consult to airlines, pilots, passengers, and medical examiners of pilots at an early stage, to help bring more psychological knowledge, more elucidation, to this field. So I think that we can conceptualize the role of the clinical aerospace psychologist as helping to plan interventions when there are already existing mental health problems *and* to help prevent mental health problems from developing in the first place. These could be two general arenas for the aerospace psychologist.

RB: There is already a European Association for Aviation Psychology and a similar organization in the United States. Many psychologists in these associations have an occupational/ergonomics interest rather than a clinical one. I'm not convinced that there is such an abundance of work that warrants a whole sub-speciality, so I think it would be helpful to have mental health practitioners who have some specialist knowledge of the presenting problems within the aerospace industry. To talk of a whole sub-speciality might be premature at this point.

BK: If we think in terms of clinical aerospace psychologists providing interventions where there is a suspected problem or a known mental health problem, it seems to me there are several arenas, some of which have been covered in the book.

One would be during the assessment or diagnosis of mental health problems in pilots; the other would be in providing psychological counselling or psychotherapy for pilots, cabin crew, or ground staff, either because of their own private life difficulties or because they have been involved in some traumatic work-related incident. We have a diagnostic function and we have a treatment function, and those would be two of the roles that clinicians might play, as well as providing treatment for passengers who suffer from overt fear of flying or who experience episodes of air rage.

RB: I would add to that very comprehensive list two other categories. One would be extending the same interventions to those people who work in the industry who are often "left out of the loop" when it comes to providing medical care, such as air traffic controllers, who have a stressful job, as well as ground maintenance engineers, many of whom have enormous responsibilities when it comes to repairing and maintaining aircraft. A high proportion of them work antisocial hours, which increases risk of dislocation from their own family and support network and also of poor work performance, which could, in turn, lead to incidents and accidents. The second group would be the family and/or care-givers of all the groups we've already spoken about. As we know, many mental health interventions are focused on the individuals, and although I think we would all accept that a good clinician would take a detailed family history and would want to assess the impact of a problem or symptom on a wider social or kin network, we are not as good at offering family, couples', or group sessions.

BK: What you said is really striking, especially when you extended our list. The different types of people who might be recipients of clinical aerospace psychology interventions now include pilots, cabin crew, air traffic controllers, ground maintenance staff, passengers, as well as the families of all the above. That is potentially a very broad group of people. And yet I have never had anyone from any of these groups come to see me in either private practice or in the public sector. I think that many in the airline industry may not be familiar with mental health settings. One might speculate—although it is only speculation—that people who are attracted to spending a lot of their time in the air might be people who have some wish to engage in flight activities: "flight" not only from the ground but "flight" from their own problems. I have never heard any colleague's presentation about treatment of a pilot or treatment of an air traffic controller: perhaps this is a group we do not get to see in the same proportion that we do, for example, businessmen, artists, musicians, or students. It seems to me that we have a fertile population of people who may be experiencing psychological difficulties and yet who do not know how to access that treatment or may not even recognize that the treatment might be helpful . . .

RB: I would suggest that there are a number of reasons for that. Let us start with what is positive. This is a fairly robust group from a psychological perspective. I don't believe that airline work attracts large numbers of people who are psychologically vulnerable or who have overt problems. There are many different stages at which they would be screened out, and their inappropriate interest would be rebuffed. Most work in the airline industry is teamwork, even though an individual's performance is important. Ultimately teamwork is the context in which it is operationalized, and for that reason there are always other people around who are observing or monitoring your work. If you are not a team player, or you bring to the work setting quite serious interpersonal psychological problems, you will stand out and risk alienation. It is an industry with a very good safety record. Another reason is that it may attract people who, perhaps much like those in other professions—surgeons, for example—are very skilful and technically minded but who don't necessarily see their forte or their primary interest as being people-orientated. They may be more interested and focused on technical or operational matters, while a focus on communication and relationships may be of secondary importance.

A further reason is that some people who work professionally in the airline industry have a fairly negative view of psychology and mental health practice. This may be through bad experience, folklore, or simply a perception that psychology doesn't have anything positive to say to the individual as it is used to serve the airline's interests and for selecting people out of jobs or for identifying problems. This is an unfortunate perception. Contrary to some popular wisdom, there are some very well-paid pilots, but if you look at the industry as a whole, a lot of people are paid an average-to-low wage. Those captains of advanced commercial jets who work for big international carriers may do very well financially, but your average worker is going to earn considerably less and may not have the resources to even consider private psychological treatment. They may also find that when going to National Health Service facilities, they encounter waiting lists. In an industry where mental health problems may threaten safe operations, a lengthy wait to see a specialist gives cause for concern. The last would be the anxiety that some may experience—particularly pilots and air traffic controllers—that, if it is discovered that they are accessing psychological care and treatment, this may affect their employment. This fear of being "discovered" may deter someone who needs to see a mental health professional from doing so.

BK: I remember one of my mentors in psychotherapy mentioning to me that the three most difficult groups of patients to engage in on-going psychotherapeutic treatment are medical students, nursing students, and actors. This is because they have peripatetic shift timetables and it is very difficult to commit to a regular session every Thursday at 4 o'clock or every Friday at 3 o'clock. It seems to me that one could readily add pilots, aircrew, air traffic controllers, ground maintenance staff, and their families to that list. A life in aviation has elements of unreliability, unpredictability, and, unsurprisingly, a lack of groundedness in terms of being able to predict one's actual lifestyle, of knowing in which country or on which continent you are going to be in next Tuesday!

RB: That is absolutely correct. The challenge for us is to be flexible around *their* needs rather than vice versa. There are many examples where collaborations and interventions have failed. This is not because what we have offered has been of poor quality, but because the way in which we have offered or delivered the service has not been acceptable to the client group with which we are working. It is highly improbable that we could ever be able to agree with a pilot on a series of meetings or regular slots for psychotherapy over an extended period. Their work pattern wouldn't enable this to happen, and they would probably be faced with considerable anxiety about missing appointments. We might even erroneously interpret their difficulty with commitment! We need to find a different way to reach them that may be briefer and more flexible. Given some of the apprehension that a few may experience about seeing a mental health professional, we should probably use a therapeutic approach that is affirming and of immediate practical help to them. I have worked with some psychotherapist colleagues at trying to develop such an approach within similar settings (see Bor, Gill, Miller, & Parrott, 2003). There are many examples that I can think of, where we can offer positive and preventative-type interventions. One example could be with pilots who are about to qualify. I regularly lecture to a group of them on managing stress and disruption in their personal lives. It is not as though they have never thought of these sorts of issues before, but the reality only sets in once they have actually become engaged by an airline and then experience disruption in their personal and professional lives.

BK: What do you advise?

RB: I advise something similar to what I learnt in the field of medical family therapy from Dr Susan McDaniel in Rochester, New York, who pointed out that, when there is illness within the family, the family has to find a place for the illness and they also have to put the illness in its place. The message in aerospace operations is similar—that is, if you are going to be a pilot, the work pattern will dominate many aspects of your life, but if you allow it to dominate every aspect, including your relationships, something will be lost along the way. You may be able to allow it to take over your life in the short term, but in time this focus will take its toll. It is important for pilots to be up front with their spouses and families and to discuss their own anxieties about being away from the family as well as perhaps some of the pleasures as well. It may be the case for some people that they chose this particular job and lifestyle because of the separateness that it occasionally brings.

BK: May I be psychoanalytically provocative for a moment? In the field of psychoanalysis we use the term "flight" often preceded by the term "manic": we speak of "manic flight" when a relationship or a situation becomes too difficult, patients will flee. They will fly away, either into an internal psychic retreat by altering their mental state through drugs, or alcohol, or promiscuous sex, or they will go to the Bahamas for a year, to paint and to try to discover some new aspect of themselves, or how they feel that through a geographical solution they can achieve a psychic solution to a problem. And we know that flight does not work. Manic flight often does not work, because one takes one's psychic luggage with one. I would like to ask whether people who have a tendency or a propensity towards manic flight actually end up in a job where they take a flight every other day, and whether the very wish to work in the airline industry represents a veritable concretization of this tendency? Are these people fleeing from difficulties or complications in intimate relationships? Do they actually prefer not to see their partners or spouses on a regular basis . . . that is potentially a gross generalization, but I am posing it as a question. . . . I wonder.

RB: The terms you use are evocative, and it is an interesting metaphor. I can't say that I have sufficient experience to say that most people who work in the industry are fleeing from problems. That is a compelling idea from a therapist, but it is highly unlikely! That is not to say that that doesn't happen, but I do not recognize it on a scale where it seems like a general problem. That said, there are positive ways of looking at this process too. For some people, a journey is necessary at a particular life stage. And it may be that this then becomes their life and lifestyle, and they become trapped in that journey. Their disaffection with the job—be it piloting, or being a flight attendant, etc.—may have its roots in the fact that they actually no longer wish to "get away from it". Most people I have worked with professionally in the airline industry are actually either very "grounded" in themselves or searching for a new place to "ground" themselves. The transitions they seek are mostly healthy and reflect normal growth and everyday struggles. Yes, there are a few who exhibit signs of greater emotional distress. "Flight" from something unpleasant or emotionally hurtful might be more characteristic of flight attendants. The job provides a mix of stability in the work or peer group and instability in parts of their personal lives for a while. It is interesting that a sizeable proportion give up their work within ten years, and one of the reasons for that may well be that they either form stable relationships back home or seek greater stability in their lives. So, if anything, psychological "flight" is mostly transient. I think it is an interesting thing for us to discover more about attachment patterns among airline employees.

BK: I think that shows that we, as mental health professionals, actually know very little about the lives, backgrounds, or motivations of people who are attracted to this industry. Yet it is an industry that pretty much all of us have used or will use extensively, as passengers on plane flights.

RB: It is interesting that, perhaps in the last two to three years, we have witnessed on television quite a number of fly-on-the-wall documentaries about air travel, some to do with an airline, some to do with a particular airport. There have also been some documentaries on the life and lifestyles of pilots, what happens on board aircraft, and about passenger behaviour. We are moving to a stage where we are peeling back the façade and removing some of the mystique that we associate with air travel. It is much like, perhaps, learning a bit about the private life of a psychotherapist . . . it is intriguing to patients, but it can perhaps sometimes be quite unnerving and potentially unattractive in other ways! They recently screened a documentary showing pilots consuming large quantities alcohol while abroad and then being hardly fit to fly the plane back. There have been documentaries about pilot suicide and crashes being associated with this. A few incidents of air rage have actually been filmed showing passengers and crew in physical combat with one another. In another, we also hear some slightly sleazy comments by an airline check-in agent at Heathrow Airport, who says that he makes judgements about whether to upgrade passengers based on the size of the man's "packet". We can't hide from this image of air travel where there are sexual connotations ranging from the attractiveness of flight attendants to lewd discussion on the flight deck or some passengers' quest to join the "mile-high club". We have moved away from a kind of innocence, or pleasant mystique, about air travel. The recent events in the United States brought this new reality crashing home to us, both literally and metaphorically. I believe that we are into a new phase in air travel. Our expectations as travellers are different, and how people perceive psychotherapists, aircrew, and airline professionals is changing as well . . . it is not how things were five or ten years ago.

BK: Yes. It is not only a question of psychological curiosity but also an important question for public safety to know about the state of mind of pilots and cabin crew. Although our comments are in the realm of speculation, I think it is important to be sure about the stability, the robustness of the individuals who are attracted to this type of work. It is work that can influence the fate of our lives. We could die at the hands of these individuals if they are in a mentally compromised state, so I think the study of the mental health of airline personnel is utterly crucial. Can mental health professionals, aviation psychologists, or psychotherapists work consultatively with airlines and with pilots? Where do you think we can offer our services?

RB: In a number of ways. It is not that we bring entirely new skills to this particular field but that we bring our traditional skills to a field that is untapped when it comes to psychological and mental health input. We also have to recognize—and I put this in a traditional context—that we are working with a resistant population. So if we go into the field with "all guns blazing", no matter how insightful and interesting some of our interventions and ideas may be, we will be rejected, and we will almost certainly fail. I would firstly identify those core areas that we can work in. I would start with passengers. The reason for that is that, more than ever, many passengers are aware of their own fears associated with flying. We have a role today in providing psychological counselling services for passengers to help them to manage their anxieties. The other is with aircrew themselves. I doubt that there will ever be sufficient mental health professionals to fully serve the airline industry. It is important that those professionals who have day-to-day responsibility, such as medical examiners, have greater support and input from psychologists, so they know what to look for, how to look for it, and what to do about psychological problems. In other words, they need to perceive a multi-disciplinary team around them. Some authorized aviation medical examiners work in isolation, with little direct recourse to mental health services, unless they access it through specialists at the Civil Aviation Authority, which is possible.

BK: Could forensic psychologists and forensic psychiatrists make a contribution here, in terms of our specialist knowledge over the prediction and identification of dangerousness? The very last thing that we would want would be a dangerous pilot, a pilot with dangerous conscious or unconscious suicidal or even homicidal tendencies. How much would the average medical examiner know about the prediction of dangerousness?

RB: It is difficult to say. The prediction of dangerousness or level of threat from an individual is a very difficult thing to assess as we know, and there is always the problem of litigation. If you pull somebody "off line"—meaning that you withdraw them from a flying position—when there is perhaps a suggestion that they are mentally unstable but there is no intent or immediate threat, that could have severe legal consequences. We would have to think that one through quite carefully.

On the other hand, I think there are some areas to get involved in, and perhaps this would be the beginning of developing a collaborative relationship. One of them would be to do with helping those who train pilots to cope with a number of different aspects of their work that involve psychological factors. These range from how to manage their personal relationships to coping with jet lag, dislocation from their family, homesickness, and the stresses of medical assessments that they frequently undergo. Another would be how pilots communicate, or whether they communicate with passengers. I am not sure of your experience, but there is a tendency to reduce the amount of communication from the flight deck to passengers, and this raises the anxiety of passengers, as we have seen from some recent research. This revealed that when the flight deck door is left closed and there is minimal verbal contact from the flight deck, passenger anxiety increases. In the new area, where the flight deck door is bolted closed and where the people responsible for safely flying us will be perceived to be more remote, there will be an increased need for communication. Passengers need the reassurance that the pilots are there and that they are in control. Whatever the form of communication—whether it is an updated weather report, or an on-time announcement—it is the value in the communication with passengers that needs to be stressed.

BK: I agree. We would all hate to fly on a plane piloted by someone with extremely good social skills but very poor technical knowledge. People who have excellent technical knowledge and a willingness to improve their psychological savvy, their ability to communicate with passengers and fellow crew, would be the ideal situation. How can we get pilots and cabin crew to communicate more rather than less with passengers? For example, a few years back I took a flight that was unbelievably turbulent. The plane was going up and down and sideways, and I really did think that we were going to die. There were no announcements at all from the captain, so I had to use my observational skills in studying the air hostesses. I saw that they had sufficient experience of different types of turbulence to realize that (a) this was not a hijacking and (b) this was not perilous turbulence. It was bad but not life-threatening, and that brought me some comfort. But I had to scan for visual clues from the flight attendants. It would have been incredibly helpful if the Captain of the plane had spoken, if only for five seconds, and said something like, "Ladies and gentlemen, this is particularly bad turbulence, but it *is only* turbulence, and we will see you through this" — the same way that a parent offers reassurance and comfort to the troubled and anxious child.

RB: You are absolutely right. There are deterrents to in-flight verbal communication. One is the perception among pilots that this is an intrusion into the passengers' desire for quiet and calm on board. This is derived from surveys among business and first-class passengers who are their premium flyers. A preference among them is to be left alone so that they can have privacy, no distractions, and can get on with their own work. But we all know that even for the most seasoned traveller it is still an unfamiliar environment. I think what tends to happen is that the flight crew and the cabin crew tend to make an assumption that people may either be frequent flyers or that they may appear docile and that they are coping well. And that is a pity, because they may misread the situation. Most people who are anxious on board aircraft tend to withdraw and endure the unpleasant feelings alone rather than become visibly agitated and display other signs of their distress.

BK: Of course. We know only too well from working with survivors of various traumas, such as rape or war, that often one of the first cognitive capacities to disappear is the capacity for verbalization. People become literally stony silent with fear and cannot ask for help precisely at the moment they most need it. I know of a child patient who had been trapped in an earthquake and came up from the earthquake totally mutistic (Dermen, 2002). I think that a lot of passengers are often immobilized by such crippling fear. Even asking a flight attendant "Is this turbulence" or "Are we going to crash?" becomes a very difficult question. I think we need to alert cabin crew that these may be the overt clinical or, in fact, sub-clinical anxieties of most passengers. I wonder as well, Robert, whether air rage might actually represent the extremes of terror of being in a life-or-death situation and that one way more volatile passengers might handle the fear of being suspended at 35,000 feet in the care of somebody else who is not communicating with you is to go mad by having an air rage attack.

RB: That is an interesting idea. We have yet to study the minds of so-called air rage perpetrators, and there are various reasons for this, not least of which is those pertaining to litigation and just having access to perpetrators. A number of people have speculated as to why passengers should want to endanger an aircraft or disrupt a flight. While each situation is unique, there are also commonalties. It may well be that there is a link between all these different situations. Some fear being entrapped, being at the mercy of someone unknown to them, and perhaps feeling infantilized or resenting how they have been communicated with, and this has led to acting-out behaviour. The other side of it is that many of these people have a history of antisocial behaviour, and, in certain conditions when they are not in control, they will act out violently, either verbally or physically.

BK: That is such a fascinating area. Given that a certain number of passengers will inevitably have had a history of antisocial behaviour, what we have to tell the airline industry is that because we cannot screen people for their criminal histories before letting them on board, what the airlines need to learn is that the potentiality for criminal acts can either be contained or exacerbated, depending on the psychological atmosphere created on board.

RB: Those are very good points. My experience is that the airline industry has actually been quite slow in their response, and containment has only recently become part of the agenda. The issue of exacerbation is not entertained by many managers in the airline industry. The belief is that passengers pay good money, take their seats, and are then expected to behave in a reasonable way and comply with all the instructions. That is an interesting belief, but it is not borne out in the reality of air travel. There have always been passengers who have misbehaved on planes and an increasing number who act aggressively. Airlines are not keen to look at the behaviour and actions of their own crew in exacerbating situations, and there are certainly a number of cases where their crews' poor management of a particular incident on a plane has probably made it worse. That said, a zero-tolerance approach to any acting-out behaviour on board an aircraft is a necessary one because, unless all passengers are aware of the penalties and the consequences of this kind of behaviour, these acts will continue. However, we don't really fully understand all of the relationship dynamics that take place at 35,000 feet that may maintain or exacerbate—or, for that matter, eliminate—the threat of air rage, and that is another important area on which those with a mental health interest can shed light.

BK: You see, I think that we, as mental health workers, underestimate how radical Sigmund Freud's concept of the talking cure remains even today. We take it for granted that any psychological intervention that we provide, whether we are psychologists or psychotherapists or counsellors or whatever, involves talking and helping our clients or patients to develop a richer vocabulary so that difficult emotions, difficult affects, can be transformed into words rather than into self-destructive or other-destructive actions. I think that even encouraging pilots to engage in simple speech-intensifying acts, such as talking to passengers, or training cabin crew, for example, to help passengers who fight with one another to talk out the situation would be of help. Although we regard this as common sense or perhaps old hat, I think we underestimate how important the encouragement of simple talking can be in a potentially life-threatening situation such as in an aircraft.

RB: One thing that binds all of us together, as therapists and mental health practitioners, is the fact that we're all persuaded that talking solves problems wherever they have been identified. . . .

And effective dialogue must involve listening too. Therapy has to be a unique personal encounter. Broadcasting relaxation skills to passengers over their headsets or in the in-flight entertainment system is insufficient. On the other hand, it would probably be inconceivable (though quite popular!) to have a therapist or a psychologist on board to talk people through their particular stresses and worries and provide a programme of relaxation that has been has been personalized—maybe something that is more interactive, somewhere between those two positions, could still be useful to passengers.

BK: And one wonders as well whether airline cabin crew could also be encouraged to initiate contact with passengers in non-practical ways. I wonder what it would do to the anxiety level on an airline carrier if flight attendants went up to each passenger and said, "are you enjoying your flight, sir? Are you enjoying your flight, madam? Is there anything I can do for you?" rather than coming around with a trolley to say "chicken or beef" or "do you want duty-frees"—to ask a more open-ended question, actually, that does not involve a practical answer, just to see if one can try to root out any problems or difficulties. Now that might seem utopian or fanciful, but I wonder whether by the simple encouragement of conversation by each passenger, during the lulls between the film and the main course, for example, whether promoting talking in that way could occur?

RB: That's a good idea. I think that the difficulty arises in terms of the pressure of the job. Their task is one of being there primarily for people's safety and, as a secondary task, the one of serving and attending to people's needs. The term "flight attendant" is not really a valid job title for many of these people. The pressure of work prevents this from happening because of the multitude of duties that attendants have to be involved in. But you are absolutely right that simply personalizing attention would decrease anxiety. I remember sitting on one flight at an emergency exit with a flight attendant sitting opposite me in one of the jump seats. The woman sitting next to me was seriously anxious, and this was picked up on by the flight attendant sitting opposite us. The flight attendant asked the woman if she was "OK", and the passenger said "no", she was feeling very anxious. The flight attendant said "don't worry, we also sometimes get a bit anxious", and it was quite remarkable how the anxiety of that passenger completely dissipated through that very brief interchange. There was no false reassurance; there was just respect and acknowledgement of the fear that that person had.

BK: And I wonder, following on from that, whether educating cabin crew into realizing that, not only can passengers suffer from overt air rage and fear of flying and panic attacks, but from sub-clinical anxiety as well. This does not usually become verbalized, but each passenger experiences a private madness in his or her own head. Cabin crew could better understand that (a) they have a parental transferential role, as lookers-after of passengers, and that (b) passengers are people who are often travelling alone, away from loved ones, or away from familiar structures, and who are also leaving familiar territory and are in transit from one situation to another, perhaps between jobs, perhaps between meetings, perhaps between relationships, and it might be that the act of travelling might help put passengers in a more vulnerable state. I think that if we could help, by even providing just a simple seminar with psychologists or psychotherapists to assist pilots and particularly the cabin crew to realize the potential vulnerability of passengers at that particular moment, I think that that would be so useful. Back in 1957, Donald Winnicott gave a lecture for midwives, and he said that the woman in stirrups, on the verge of delivering her baby, may in fact be the head of a major corporation, highly competent in her own right. But at this moment, she has become vulnerable and dependent, and thus the midwife must look after her (Winnicott, 1957a, 1957b). And I would suggest that each of us as passengers experiences a different degree of vulnerability. We lose part of our competencies, whether we want to admit this consciously or not; we are being flown by somebody else, we are not flying the plane, and I think if we can help the air personnel to realize the parental, transferential role that they adopt in our minds and in our reality, that that might help to change their attitude towards passengers.

RB: There isn't enough psychologically oriented material that is discussed with people in their busy training schedules, be it cabin or flight-deck crew, and I think we can make a case for increasing it without this turning into a psychotherapy training! What you say is also borne out in research: we know that in aircraft accidents, when passengers have to leave or escape from the aircraft as quickly as possible, many will turn to, and rely on, flight attendants to guide them out. These flight attendants are trained literally to yell at passengers, some of whom become immobilized at that very terrifying moment. That role, of the parental figure, of somebody in control, is a very important one, particularly in emergency situations. Even when the flight is going well, we still look to others to provide a degree of structure and safety, and that is a very important thing. Unfortunately, the popular image of flight attendants may partly undermine that kind of professionalism with which we want to hold figures in.

BK: Hmm. You are right that it would be inappropriate and complicated to offer a full psychological training to a flight attendant, but in terms of increasing their psychological sensitivity, I think that could be quite helpful, and I also wonder what we could offer by way of psychological support to the cabin crew to help them deal with what must be their annoyance with passengers. I was very shocked, Robert, when you told me some time ago that some pilots casually refer to passengers as "self-loading cargo", which seems to me a highly contemptuous and derogatory way of describing paying air-line passengers. If you are a flight attendant and you have to look after 250 passengers, let us say you have 8 or 10 others to help you, however many are in your designated area, you might have suddenly inherited for that 6-hour flight to America 20 new children who need to go to the loo, who need to have their dinners and their special meals, and extra blankets and pillows, and so on and so on. They are asking you for pens and paper and their headphones don't work . . . in a way, the flight attendants become very much like mothers whose infants make continual bodily demands on them. I would imagine that, although aircrew are being paid for this, they also experience tremendous unconscious or conscious hatred towards the passengers. And I wonder, do they have a space to take these anxieties to, do they have a supervision group, do they have a support group, just as we would do as clinicians?

RB: They may chat among themselves about their experience of a flight, but there isn't a structured, well-organized, or facilitated context in which to do this. You raise an interesting example of flight attendants having to manage and care for children. If you interviewed flight attendants in the way that we have in our own research, they would allude to the fact that passengers regress psychologically as soon as they get on board the flight. Some become juvenile; they become attention-seeking, and within moments a sense of entitlement sets in that can be quite annoying on a good day and soul-destroying on a bad day. They will tell you that there is nothing like an ungracious passenger who cannot see that it is not flight attendants' fault that their meal has not been loaded, their headset doesn't work, the movie is jumping, or they haven't been seated with their family, unpleasant as all of these experiences may be. Because they are the immediate public face of the airline and representatives of the airline, they are the people who must bear the brunt. There are certain expectations between crew and passengers. Sadly, crew don't get the chance to reflect on psychological processes in their work in a structured context. The closest they may come to doing so is on the crew bus or around the pool of the hotel they are staying at.

BK: It might alter the experiences of cabin crew dramatically if, after each flight, they all congregated in some room in the airport rather than going to the bar, for example, where they could have even a 20-minute discussion about how they managed the flight, were there any difficult passengers, how did they deal with it, sharing experiences ...

RB: It is an interesting idea, but I think, much like passengers, most want to leave the airport, get home, or reach their final destination, and turn their back on their work. That said, I think that there is a place for doing it every few flights, briefly before flights, and as part of their initial training.

BK: It would have to be facilitated by someone who is expert at these matters, and I am thinking what tremendous insights the Hungarian psychoanalyst Michael Balint had when he realized that general medical practitioners need to have discussion groups to talk about the impact of their very difficult patients. You and I have both taught at the Royal Free Hospital Medical School. Teaching medical students, we know how important it is to give medical students a space, a structured space, in which they can talk about their clinical work, and perhaps aircrew also need a space of this kind, like a group for airline workers.

RB: Absolutely. It is also a way of helping them debrief so that complex feelings are not taken away or carried home with them. It might also help to improve their sense of professionalism and bring greater clarity to their role, thereby reducing staff turnover.

Brett, I wanted to ask you if you had any final thoughts about mental health, aviation, and the future?

BK: Final thoughts? Well, I think that clinical aerospace psychology is a new and potentially exciting area. In view of the catastrophic events of 11 September 2001, the meaning of flying, even among those of us who had been seasoned travellers and had not really given a second thought to the potential dangerousness of aircraft, have suddenly become aware of the possible terrors. For the foreseeable future, there will be passengers who are more anxious, pilots who are more anxious, and it may be that we will need to be more proactive as mental health professionals in making our services known. We do know something about working with anxiety, containing and alleviating anxiety, and helping organizations through organizational consultation to create a more sensitive working environment. I think that if we can help airline employees to create a better working environment, the crew will be happier and feel more contained, and passengers will pick this up, and I think air rage and other problems could be minimized.

RB: I also think it is an exciting and interesting area in which mental health practice can be introduced. This is a new and challenging context into which mental health practice can expand and a relationship that has effectively never properly "taken off" can be developed. Out of adversity and tragedy has come a keen interest in mental health processes across the spectrum associated with air travel. The challenge for all of us will be to do so in a way that fits with the lifestyle and the unique needs of both client groups—passengers as well as the ground and aircrew. I hope that some of the ideas that we have written about will stimulate the interest of readers to become more involved so that we can better understand the problems and consult more widely. Although we may sometimes use different language as mental health practitioners and choose to focus on different levels of intrapsychic and interpersonal systems, the concepts are actually very similar. I have learnt more about psychodynamic concepts applied to the experience of travellers and pilots through our conversations. So, thanks to you too!

BK: Thank you.

REFERENCES

American Psychiatric Association (1987). *Diagnostic and Statistical Manual of Mental Disorders* (DSM-III-R) (3rd ed.). Washington, DC: American Psychiatric Association.

American Psychiatric Association (1994). *Diagnostic and Statistical Manual of Mental Disorders* (DSM-IV). Washington, DC: American Psychiatric Association.

Anderson, H. (1919). *The Medical and Surgical Aspects of Aviation.* London: Oxford University Press and Hodder & Stoughton.

Anthony, E. (1988). Psychiatry. In: J. Ernsting & P. King (Eds.), *Aviation Medicine* (2nd ed.). London: Butterworths.

Bandura, A. (1977). Self-efficacy: Toward a unifying theory of behaviour change. *Psychological Review, 84*: 191–215.

Beh, H., & McLaughlin, P. (1991). Mental performance of air crew following layovers on transzonal flights. *Ergonomics, 34*: 123–135.

Bell, P., Greene, T., Fisher, J., & Baum, A. (1996). *Environmental Psychology.* New York: Harcourt Brace.

Bennett, G. (1983). Psychiatric disorders in civilian pilots. *Aviation, Space and Environmental Medicine, 54* (7): 588–589.

Beny, A., Paz, A., & Potasman, I. (2001). Psychiatric problems in returning travelers: Features and associations. *Journal of Travel Medicine, 8*: 243–246.

Bor, R. (1999). Unruly passenger behaviour and in-flight violence: A psychological perspective. *Travel Medicine International, 17* (1): 5–10.

Bor, R. (Ed.) (2003a). *Passenger Behaviour.* Aldershot: Ashgate.

Bor, R. (2003b). Trends in disruptive passenger behaviour on board UK registered aircraft: 1999–2003. *Travel Medicine and Infectious Disease, 1*: 153–157.

Bor, R., Gill, S., Miller, R., & Parrott, C. (2003). *Doing Therapy Briefly.* Hampshire: Palgrave.

Bor, R., Josse, J., & Palmer, S. (2000). *Stress Free Flying.* Salisbury, Wilts.: Quay Books.

Bor, R., Russell, M., Parker, J., & Papadopoulos, L. (2001). Survey of the world's airlines about managing disruptive passengers. *International Civil Aviation Organisation Journal, 56* (2): 21–30.

Bor, R., & Van Gerwen, L. (Eds.) (2003). *Psychological Perspectives on the Treatment of Fear of Flying.* Aldershot: Ashgate.

Borrill, J., & Iljon Foreman, E. (1996). Understanding cognitive change: A qualitative study of cognitive-behavioural therapy on fear of flying. *Clinical Psychology and Psychotherapy, 3* (1): 62–75.

Bowles, S., Ursin, M., & Picano, J. (2000). Aircrew perceived stress: Examining crew performance, crew position and captains' personality. *Aviation, Space and Environmental Medicine, 71* (11): 1093–1097.

Brooks, N., & McKinley, W. (1992). Mental health consequences of the Lockerbie Disaster. *Journal of Traumatic Stress, 5* (4): 527–543.

Butcher, J., Morfitt, R., Rouse, S., & Holden, R. (1997). Reducing MMPI-2 defensiveness: The effect of specialized instructions on retest validity in job applicant samples. *Journal of Personality Assessment, 68* (2): 385–401.

Caldwell, J. (1997). Fatigue in the aviation environment: An overview of the causes and effects as well as recommended countermeasures. *Aviation, Space and Environmental Medicine, 68* (10): 932–938.

Cho, K. (2001). Chronic "jet lag" produces temporal lobe atrophy and spatial cognitive deficits. *Nature Neuroscience, 4* (6): 567–568.

Chung, M., Easthope, Y., Chung, C., & Clark-Carter, D. (1999). The relationship between trauma and personality in victims of the Boeing 737-2D6C crash in Coventry. *Journal of Clinical Psychology, 55* (5): 617–629.

Chung, M., Easthope, Y., Eaton, B., & McHugh, C. (1999). Describing traumatic responses and distress of community residents directly and indirectly exposed to an aircraft crash. *Psychiatry, 62*: 125–137.

Cloninger, C., Svrakic, D., Bayon, C., & Prezybeck, T. (1997). Personality disorders. In S. B. Guze (Ed.), *Adult Psychiatry* (pp. 301–317). Seattle, WA: Washington University, Mosby.

Cook, C. (1997a). Aircrew alcohol and drug policies: A survey of commercial airlines. *International Journal of Drug Policy, 8* (3): 153–160.

Cook, C. (1997b). Alcohol and aviation. *Addiction, 92* (5): 539–555.

Cooper, C., & Sloan, S. (1985a). Occupational and psychosocial stress among commercial aviation pilots. *Journal of Occupational Medicine, 27* (8): 570–576.

Cooper, C., & Sloan, S. (1985b). The sources of stress on the wives of commercial airline pilots. *Aviation, Space and Environmental Medicine, 56*: 317–321.

Cullen, S. (1998). Aviation suicide: A review of general aviation accidents in the U.K., 1970–96. *Aviation, Space and Environmental Medicine, 69*: 969–968.

Dahlberg, A. (2001). *Air Rage: An Underestimated Safety Risk.* Aldershot: Ashgate.

Dean, R., & Whitaker, K. (1982). Fear of flying: Impact on U.S. air travel industry. *Journal of Travel Research, 21*: 7–17.

Denison, D., Ledwith, F., & Poulton, E. (1966). Complex reaction times at simulated cabin altitudes of 5000 feet and 8000 feet. *Aerospace Medicine, 37*: 1010–1013.

Dermen, S. (2002). Psychoanalytic perspectives on traumatized children: The Armenia experience. In: B. Kahr (Ed.), *The Legacy of Winnicott: Essays on Infant and Child Mental Health* (pp. 100–116). London: Karnac.

Diener, E. (1980). Deindividuation: The absence of self-awareness and self regulation in group members. In P. Paulus (Ed.), *The Psychology of Group Influence.* Hillside, NJ. Lawrence Erlbaum.

Doctor, R., McVarish, C., & Boone, R. (1990). Long-term behavioral treatment effects for the fear of flying. *Phobia Practice and Research Journal, 3* (1): 33–42.

Edwards, M., & Edwards, E. (1990). *The Aircraft Cabin: Managing the Human Factors.* Brookfield VT: Gower Technical.

Ekeberg, O., Kjeldsen, E., Greenwood, D., & Enger, E. (1990). Correlations between psychological and physiological responses to acute flight phobia. *Scandinavian Journal of Clinical Laboratory Investigation, 50:* 671–677.

Festinger, L. (1957). *Theory of Cognitive Dissonance.* San Francisco, CA: Stanford University Press.

Flynn, C., Sturges, M., Swarsen, R., & Kohn, G. (1993). Alcoholism and treatment in airline aviators: One company's results. *Aviation, Space and Environmental Medicine, 64:* 314–318.

Foushee, H. (1984). Dyads and triads at 35,000 feet: Factors affecting group process and aircrew performance. *American Psychologist, 39:* 886–893.

Foushee, H., & Manos, K. (1981). Information transfer within the cockpit: Problems of intracockpit communications. In: C. Billings & E. Cheaney (Eds.), *Information Transfer Problems in the Aviation System.* NASA Report TP-1875. Moffett Field, CA: NASA-Ames Research Center (NTIS No. N81-31162).

Fowlie, D., & Aveline, M. (1985). The emotional consequences of ejection, rescue and rehabilitation in RAF aircrew. *British Journal of Psychiatry, 146:* 609–613.

Fraley, R., & Shaver, P. (1998). Airport separations: A naturalistic study of adult attachment dynamics of separating couples. *Journal of Personality and Social Psychology, 75* (5): 1198–1211.

Freedman, J. (1975). *Crowding and Behaviour.* San Francisco, CA. Freeman Press.

Gersons, B., & Carlier, I. (1993). Plane crash crisis intervention: A preliminary report from the Bijlmermeer, Amsterdam. *Crisis, 14* (3): 109–116.

Giles, D., & Lochridge, G. (1985). Behavioral airsickness management program for student pilots. *Aviation, Space and Environmental Medicine, 56*: 991–994.

Harris, D. (2002). Drinking and flying: Causes, effects and the development of effective countermeasures. *Human Factors and Aerospace Safety, 2* (4): 297–317.

Helmreich, R. (1987). Exploring flight crew behaviour. *Social Behaviour, 2*: 63–72.

Helmreich, R. (2000). On error management: Lessons from aviation. *British Medical Journal, 320*: 781–785.

Holdener, F. (1993). Alcohol and civil aviation. *Addiction, 88*: 953–958.

Iljon Foreman, E., & Borrill, J. (1994). The freedom to fly: A long-term follow-up of three cases of fear of flying. *Journal of Travel Medicine, 1* (1): 30–35.

Jauhar, P., & Weller, M. (1982). Psychiatric morbidity and time zone changes: A study of patients from Heathrow Airport. *British Journal of Psychiatry, 140*: 231–235.

Johnston, A., & Kelly, M. (1988). Post accident/incident counseling: Some exploratory findings. *Aviation, Space and Environmental Medicine, 59*: 766–769.

Jones, D., & Marsh, R. (2001). Psychiatric considerations in military aerospace medicine. *Aviation, Space and Environmental Medicine, 72*: 129–135.

Jones, D., Katchen, M., Patterson, J., & Rea, M. (1997). Neuropsychiatry in aerospace medicine. In: R. DeHart (Ed.), *Fundamentals of Aerospace Medicine*. Baltimore, MD: Williams & Wilkins.

Karlins, M., Koh, F., & McCully, L. (1989). The spousal factor in pilot stress. *Aviation, Space and Environmental Medicine, 60*: 1112–1115.

Kryter, K. (1990). Aircraft noise and social factors in psychiatric hospital admission rates: A re-examination of some data. *Psychological Medicine, 20*: 395–411.

Lane, P., & Bor, R. (2002). Cabin crew experiences and perceptions of "air rage". *International Journal of Applied Aviation Studies, 2* (2): 57–70.

Leather, P., Brady, C., Lawrence, C., Beale, D., & Cox, T. (1999).

Work-Related Violence: Assessment and Intervention. London: Routledge.

Livesley, W. J. (2001). Conceptual and Taxonomic Issues. In: W. J. Livesley (Ed.), *Handbook of Personality Disorders: Theory, Research and Treatment.* New York: Guildford Press.

Lundin, T. (1995). Transportation disasters: A review. *Journal of Traumatic Stress, 8* (3): 381–389.

Matsumoto, K., & Goebert, D. (2001). In-flight psychiatric emergencies. *Aviation, Space and Environmental Medicine, 72* (10): 919–923.

Modell, J., & Mountz, J. (1990). Drinking and flying: The problem of alcohol use by pilots. *New England Journal of Medicine, 323* (7): 455–461.

Muir, H., & Marrison, C. (1989). Human factors in cabin safety. *Aerospace* (April): 18–22.

Patterson, J., Jones, D., Marsh, R., & Drummund, F. (2001). Aeromedical management of US Air Force aviators who attempt suicide. *Aviation, Space and Environmental Medicine, 72*: 1081–1085.

Picano, J., & Edwards, H. (1996). Psychiatric syndromes associated with problems in aeronautical adaptation among military student pilots. *Aviation, Space and Environmental Medicine, 67*: 1119–1123.

Price, W., & Holley, D. (1990). Shiftwork and safety in aviation. *Occupational Medicine, 5* (2): 343–377.

Raschmann, J., Patterson, J., & Schofield, G. (1990). A retrospective study of marital discord in pilots: The USAFSAM experience. *Aviation, Space and Environmental Medicine, 61*: 1145–1148.

Reason, J. (1974). *Man in Motion: The Psychology of Travel.* New York: Walker & Co.

Reinhart, R. (1997). *FAA Medical Certification: Guidelines for Pilots.* Ames, IA: Iowa State University Press.

Rigg, R., & Cosgrove, M. (1994). Aircrew wives and the intermittent husband syndrome. *Aviation, Space and Environmental Medicine, 65*: 654–660.

Roberts, R. (1989). Passenger fear of flying: Behavioural treatment with extensive in-vivo exposure and group support. *Aviation, Space and Environmental Medicine, 60*: 342–348.

Rothbaum, B., Hodges, L., Smith, S., Lee, J., & Price, L. (2000). A controlled study of virtual reality exposure therapy for the fear of flying. *Journal of Consulting and Clinical Psychology, 68* (6): 1020–1026.

Rotten, J. (1987). Hemmed in and hating it: Effects of shape of room on tolerance for crowding. *Perceptual and Motor Skills, 64*: 285–286.

Senechal, P., & Traweek, A. (1988). The aviation psychology program at RAF Upper Heyford. *Aviation, Space and Environmental Medicine, 59*: 973–975.

Slagle, D., Reichman, M., Rodenhauser, P., Knoedler, D., & Davis, C. (1990). Community psychological effects following a non-fatal aircraft accident. *Aviation, Space and Environmental Medicine, 61* (10): 879–886.

Sloan, S., & Cooper, C. (1986). Stress coping strategies in commercial airline pilots. *Journal of Occupational Medicine, 23* (1): 49–52.

Smith, R. (1983). Psychiatric disorders as they relate to aviation: The problem in perspective. *Aviation, Space and Environmental Medicine, 54* (7): 586–587.

Strongin, T. (1987). A historical review of the fear of flying among aircrewmen. *Aviation, Space and Environmental Medicine, 58*: 263–267.

Terr, L., Bloch, D., Michel, B., Hong Shi, M., Reinhardt, J., & Metayer, S. (1997). Children's thinking in the wake of *Challenger. American Journal of Psychiatry, 154* (6): 744–751.

Thompson, J. (1991). Kuwait Airways hijack: Psychological consequences for survivors. *Stress Medicine, 7*: 3–9.

Tyrer, P., Casey, P. R., & Ferguson, B. (1993). Personality disorder in perspective. In: P. Tyrer & G. Stein (Eds.), *Personality Disorder Reviewed.* London: Gaskell/Royal College of Psychiatrists.

Van Gerwen, L., Spinhoven, P., Van Dyck, R., & Diekstra, R. (1999). Construction and psychometric characteristics of two self-report questionnaires for the assessment of a fear of flying. *Psychological Assessment, 11* (2): 146–158.

Van Tilburg, M., Vingerhoets, A., & van Heck, G. (1996). Homesickness: A review of the literature. *Psychological Medicine, 26*: 899–912.

Walk, R. D. (1979). Depth perception and a laughing heaven. In: A. D. Pick (Ed.), *Perception and Its Development: A Tribute to Eleanor J. Gibson* (pp. 63–87). Hillsdale, NJ: Lawrence Erlbaum Associates.

Waterhouse, J., Reilly, T., & Atkinson, G. (1997). Jet-lag. *Lancet, 350*: 1611–1616.

Winefield, A. (1995). Unemployment: Its psychological costs. In: C. Cooper & I. Robertson (Eds.), *International Review of Industrial and Organisational Psychology, 10*. London: John Wiley.

Winnicott, D. W. (1957a). The contribution of psycho-analysis to midwifery. Part I. *Nursing Mirror and Midwives Journal* (17 May): xi–xii.

Winnicott, D. W. (1957b). The contribution of psycho-analysis to midwifery. Part II. *Nursing Mirror and Midwives Journal* (24 May): 553–554.

Winnicott, D. W. (1967). Preliminary notes for "Communication Between Infant and Mother, Mother and Infant, Compared and Contrasted". In: D. W. Winnicott, *Babies and Their Mothers* (pp. 107–109), ed. C. Winnicott, R. Shepherd, & M. Davis. Reading, MA: Addison-Wesley, 1987.

Winnicott, D. W. (1968). Communication between infant and mother, mother and infant, compared and contrasted. In: W. G. Joffe (Ed.), *What Is Psychoanalysis?* (pp. 15–25). London: Baillière, Tindall & Cassell.

Wolpe, J. (1958). *Psychotherapy by Reciprocal Inhibition*. San Francisco, CA: Stanford University Press.

Zuckerman, J. (Ed.). (2001). *Principles and Practice of Travel Medicine*. Chichester: John Wiley.

INDEX

accidents, air: *see* air accidents
acrophobia, 12
acting-out behaviour, 24, 87–88
  passengers', 74
    examples, 26–27
  pilots', 50
aero-neurosis, 43
aerospace, mental health issues in,
  76
affective disorders, 45
agoraphobia, 15
Air Botswana crash (1998), 58
air accidents, 18, 53
  passenger responses to, 29–33
  pilot reactions to, 52–54
  survivors of, 3, 53, 73
aircraft cabin, environment of,
  25
aircrew (*passim*):
  fears and anxieties of, 3
  mental health issues of, 71
  –passenger relationships, 4, 28–
  31

  psychological problems among,
    39, 46–49
  selection of, 3, 62
  testing of, 62
airline industry:
  economic repercussions of
    terrorist actions, 40
  psychological consultation to,
    ergonomic aspects of, 2
air marshals, 61
air pressure, low, 25
air rage, 14, 23–28, 69, 74, 77, 83,
  88, 90, 94
  and history of antisocial
    behaviour, 24
  perpetrators of, mentality of, 87
airsickness:
  management, 60
  pilots', 60
air traffic controllers, 11, 41, 75, 77,
  79
  and pilots, communication
    between, 2

air travel, physiological and
        health-related aspects of,
        3
alcohol, 22, 45, 50
    dependency/alcoholism, 4, 54
        pilots', 44
    misuse, 14, 63
        by pilots, 41, 45, 48–49, 54–
        57
    use, 9, 14, 37
        pilots', 43, 55
American Psychiatric Association,
        49
Anderson, H., 43
Anthony, E., 46
anticipatory anxiety, 16, 18, 68
antidepressants, dependence on,
        45
antimalarials, 4
antisocial behaviour, 24, 87
        pilots', 48
antisocial personality patterns,
        74
anxiety:
    anticipatory, 68
    disorder, 41
    hierarchy, 19
    phobic, 67
    physiological symptoms of,
        management of, 18
    sub-clinical, 90
anxiolytic medication, 23
Atkinson, G., 32
attachment patterns, impact of
        travel on, 3, 8, 33–34, 68
Aveline, M., 53
aversive conditioning, 16
aviation doctor, 41
Aviation Medical Examiner
        (AME), 48, 64
avoidance, 8, 13, 17, 20, 23
    behaviours, 16

Balint, M., 93
Bandura, A., 18

Baum, A., 25
Bayon, C., 50
Beale, D., 28
Beh, H., 25
behavioural disturbance, 49
Bell, P., 25
Bennett, G., 47, 48
Beny, A., 4, 22
beta-blockers, 20
Bijlmermeer El Al Boeing 747
        freighter disaster,
        Amsterdam (1992), 53
bipolar disorder, 45
Bloch, D., 54
blood alcohol concentration
        (BAC), 56
Boone, R., 15, 21
Bor, R., xiii, 2, 10, 14, 22–24, 28, 71–
        94
borderline personality disorder,
        15
Borrill, J., 14, 18
Brady, C., 28
British Airways, 27, 72
Brooks, N., 53
Butcher, J., 51

Caldwell, J., 59, 60
cardiovascular disease, 47
Carlier, I., 53
Casey, P. R., 50
catastrophic thinking, 12, 13
Cho, K., 59
Chung, C., 54
Chung, M., 54
circadian desynchronization, see
        jet lag
City University, London, 73
Clark-Carter, D., 54
claustrophobia, 10, 12, 15, 25
clinical depression, 49
Cloninger, C., 50
cognitive behavioural therapy
        intervention, 17, 21
cognitive psychology, 41

cognitive restructuring, 17, 21
conduct disorder, 74
consciousness, disturbance or loss of, 45
control, sense of, 18
convulsive disorders, 45
Cook, C., 55, 56
Cooper, C., 51, 52
Cosgrove, M., 34, 51
counselling, post-incident, 3
Cox, T., 28
Cranebank, British Airways training centre, 72
crew, see aircrew
Crew Resource Management (CRM), 2, 31
Cullen, S., 57
culture, role of in in-flight stress, 25

Dahlberg, A., 27
Davis, C., 53
Dean, R., 15
death from flying, 65
deep relaxation, 20
deep-vein thrombosis, 33, 70
de-individuation, 25
dementia, 54
denial:
  of fear of flying, 66
  of possibility of death, 66
Denison, D., 25
depression, 50
  pilots', 48, 53
Dermen, S., 87
desensitization treatment, 16
  systematic, 15, 19, 20, 21
Diekstra, R., 11
Diener, E., 25
Doctor, R., 15, 21
drug misuse, 4, 25
  pilots', 48, 54–57
Drummund, F., 59

Easthope, Y., 54

Eaton, B., 54
Edwards, E., 25
Edwards, H., 48, 62
Edwards, M., 25
Egypt Air Flight 990 crash (1999), 58
Ekeberg, O., 23
El Al:
  Bijlmermeer Boeing 747 freighter disaster, Amsterdam (1992), 53
  security precautions, 61
emergencies, in-flight, psychiatric, 22
Enger, E., 23
environmental challenges, pilots', 59–60
epilepsy, 45, 54
ergonomics, 5, 41, 76
European Association for Aviation Psychology, 76
European Joint Aviation Regulation (JAR), 44, 45

fear:
  of confinement, 10
  of falling, 69
  of flying, 2, 60, 73, 74, 75, 77, 90
    causes of, 11–14
    cognitive vs. somatic symptoms of, 16
    key therapeutic features, 21–23
    as phobia, 10, 14, 65–70
    pilots', 41, 43, 52
    psychological assessment of, 14–23
    psychological treatment for, 3
    treatment of, 14–23
    see also flight phobia
  of heights, 10
Ferguson, B., 50
Festinger, L., 36
"fight-or-flight" response, 23
Fisher, J., 25

flight:
  anxiety, 14, 17
  attendants:
    as maternal substitutes, 68–70
    role confusion of, 29
  crew:
    counselling service for, 72
    problems for, 8
  deck:
    automation on, 40, 48
    cultural mix on, 47
    culture of, 4, 30
    environment, 30, 31
    instruments, improved
      layout of, 2
    "office" of pilots, 40, 72
    pilot incapacitation on, 62
  phobia, 10, 14, 16–18, 22
    treatment of, kinds of
      intervention, 18–21, 65–70
  physical principles of,
    education about, 18
  safety, 29, 41, 51
    spousal factor, 51
  simulator, 72
  surgeons, 64
Flight Anxiety Modality
    Questionnaire, 16
Flight Anxiety Situations
    Questionnaire, 15
flying:
  death from, 65
  fear of, see fear of flying
Flynn, C., 56
forensic psychiatry/psychology, 84
Foushee, H., 4, 30, 31, 40
Fowlie, D., 53
Fraley, R., 9, 34, 68
Freedman, J., 25
Freud, S., 88

gastrointestinal illness, 35
gender, role of in in-flight stress,
    25

Gersons, B., 53
Giles, D., 60
Gill, S., 80
Goebert, D., 22
Gotch, O., 43
gravitational changes, 46
Greene, T., 25
Greenwood, D., 23
ground maintenance staff, 2, 75,
    77, 79
  responsibilities of, 77

halo effect, 49
Harris, D., 55
health-care professional, role of,
    37
Helmreich, R., 30, 41, 60
hierarchical interactions, 4
HIV, 35
Hodges, L., 17
Holden, R., 51
Holdener, F., 55
Holley, D., 52, 60
homesickness, 4, 34, 85
Hong Shi, M., 54
hypnotics, dependence on, 45
hypoxia, 25, 46

Iljon Foreman, E., 14, 18
illicit drug use, 25
incidents and trauma,
    psychological reactions to,
    pilots', 39, 52–54
in-flight psychiatric emergencies,
    22
inhalers, dependence on, 45
insomnia, 8, 32
interaction(s):
  hierarchical, 4
  small-group, 4
"intermittent husband/spouse"
    relationships, 8, 34
International Civil Aviation
    Organization (ICAO), 74

Japan Airlines attempted crash
        (1982), 58
Jauhar, P., 4, 23
jet lag (circadian
        desynchronization), 2–3, 8,
        24, 31–33, 85
    flight attendants', 59
    pilots', 47, 59
Johnston, A., 54
Jones, D., 42, 45, 47, 51, 59
Josse, J., 22

Kahr, B., xiv, 65–70, 71–94
Karlins, M., 52
Katchen, M., 42
Kelly, M., 54
Kill Devil Hills, Ohio, Wright
        brothers' flight (1903), 3
Kjeldsen, E., 23
Knoedler, D., 53
Koh, F., 52
Kohn, G., 56
Kryter, K., 23

Lane, P., 24
Lawrence, C., 28
Leather, P., 28
Ledwith, F., 25
Lee, J., 17
Leonardo da Vinci, 7
Livesley, W. J., 50
Lochridge, G., 60
Lockerbie Pan Am 103 disaster
        (1988), 53
Lundin, T., 53

malaria, 35
manic defences, 66
manic flight, 81
Manos, K., 31
Mark Twain (Clemens, S.), 10
Marrison, C., 29
Marsh, R., 45, 59
Matsumoto, K., 22

McCully, L., 52
McDaniel, S., 80
McHugh, C., 54
McKinley, W., 53
McLaughlin, P., 25
McVarish, C., 15, 21
medical certification, 46, 55
    denial of, criteria for, 45–46
    pilots', 39
        loss of, 41
        psychological requirements
            for, 44–46
medication, 9, 13, 20–21, 23, 32, 35–
        36
    anxiolytic, 23
    and pilot performance, 57
mental health professionals, 1, 2,
        11, 21, 41, 62, 74, 76, 82–84,
        94
    antipathy towards, 64
    role of, 39
Metayer, S., 54
Michel, B., 54
Miller, R., 80
misconduct, pilots', 48
Modell, J., 56
Morfitt, R., 51
motion sickness, 8
Mountz, J., 56
Muir, H., 29

National Transportation Safety
        Board (NTSB), 58
nervous system:
    progressive disease of, 45
    transient loss of control of, 45
neurosis, 45
    aero-, 43
    occupational, 43

occupational neurosis, 43

Palmer, S., 22
panic attack, 12, 13, 90

Papadopoulos, L., 28
Parker, J., 28
Parrott, C., 80
passenger(s) (*passim*):
    behaviour, 7–38, 74, 82
        unruly, 23–28, 74
    –crew relationship, 4, 28–31
    hostile, 9
    mental health issues, 71
Patterson, J., 42, 52, 59
Paz, A., 4, 22
Pennsylvania, terrorist attack (11
        Sept. 2001), 1
Pentagon, terrorist attack (11 Sept.
        2001), 1, 72
personality disorder(s), 45, 48, 50
    pilots', 49–51
phobia(s), 14
    acrophobia, 12
    agoraphobia, 15
    claustrophobia, 10, 12, 15, 25
    flight, 10, 14, 16–18, 22
        treatment of, kinds of
            intervention, 18–21, 65–70
    travel, 5, 10, 14, 73
        clinics, 73
        psychodynamics of, 65–70
phobic anxiety, 67
phobic reactions, pilots', 48
physical evolution barriers, 8
Picano, J., 48, 62
pilot(s), airline:
    and air traffic controllers,
        communication between, 2
    alcohol:
        dependency/alcoholism of,
            44
        misuse by, 41, 45, 48–49, 54–
            57
        use by, 43, 55
    coping strategies of, 52
    drug misuse by, 39, 48, 54–57
    incapacitation of, on flight deck,
        62

medical certification of, 39
medical and psychological
        assessment of, 45
mental health of, 5, 39–64
as paternal substitutes, 69–70
performance of, psychological
        factors, 42
personality types of, 41
personal relationships of, effect
        on job situation, 39
psychological reactions to
        incidents and trauma, 39
reluctance of to consult with
        psychologist, 42
selection, 43–44
suicide, 19, 39, 83
    by aircraft, 57–59
post-alcohol impairment (PAI), 56
post-incident counselling, 3
post-traumatic stress disorder
        (PTSD), 53, 54, 73
Potasman, I., 4, 22
Poulton, E., 25
Prezybeck, T., 50
Price, L., 17
Price, W., 52, 60
progressive disease of nervous
        system, 45
prophylactic napping, 60
psychiatry, forensic, 84
psychoanalytic therapy, long-term
        exploratory, 21
psychodynamic analysis of flight
        phobia, 67
psychology, forensic, 84
psychological problems among
        aircrew, 39
psychology:
    aerospace, clinical, 2, 41, 64
        development of, 1–5
        future of, 71–94
        travel phobia, 65–70
psychometric testing, 4
psychosis, 45, 48, 49

PTSD: *see* post-traumatic stress
        disorder

rape, survivors of, 86
Raschmann, J., 52
Rea, M., 42
Reason, J., 7–8
reciprocal inhibition, 19
recreational and illicit drugs,
        dependence on, 13, 45
Reichman, M., 53
Reilly, T., 32
Reinhardt, J., 54
Reinhart, R., 44
relationships, impact of travel on,
        33–34, 51–52
relaxation:
    techniques, 19–20, 32, 60
    training, 17–19
"reverse culture shock", 34
Rigg, R., 34, 51
risk-taking behaviour among
        travellers, 34–38
    health, 35–36
    sexual, 36
Roberts, R., 21
Rodenhauser, P., 53
Rothbaum, B., 17
Rotten, J., 25
Rouse, S., 51
Royal Air Maroc crash (1994), 58
Royal Flying Corps, 43
Royal Free Hospital:
    Diploma in Travel Medicine, 73
    Medical School, 93
    Travel Health Clinic, London, 73
Russell, M., 28

Schofield, G., 52
secondary traumatization, 73
sedatives, dependence on, 45
self-destructive acts, 45
self-efficacy, 18
Senechal, P., 41

separation, 19
    anxiety, 68, 70
    and loss, 34, 70
sexually transmitted infections, 35
Shaver, P., 9, 34, 68
sibling rivalry, 4
Silk Air 737 crash (1997), 58
Slagle, D., 53
Sloan, S., 51, 52
small-group interaction, 4
Smith, R., 47
Smith, S., 17
somatization, pilots', 48
spatial cognitive deficits, 59
Spinhoven, P., 11
stress:
    air crews', 38
    airline employees', 4
    air traffic controllers', 77
    air travellers', 7–9, 13, 15, 18, 20,
        23–25, 27, 33–34, 37–38, 89
    inoculation training, 17
    management of, 76, 80
    pilots', 39–43, 45–47, 49–52, 54,
        55, 85
      post-incident, 41
    post-traumatic stress disorder,
        53, 73
    -susceptible personality, 13
    travel, 3
Strongin, T., 52
Sturges, M., 56
sub-clinical anxiety, 90
substance:
    dependence, 45
    misuse, 45
      by pilots, 41, 39, 45
suicide, pilots', 39
    by aircraft, 57
Svrakic, D., 50
Swarsen, R., 56

temporal lobe atrophy, 59
Terr, L., 54

terrorism:
    attack(s), 70
        of 11 September 2001, 1, 18,
            19, 40, 65, 72, 94
        threat of, responses to, 60–61
Thompson, J., 53
thought stopping, 17
tranquillizers, 67
transitional objects, 9
traumas, survivors of, 86
traumatization, secondary, 73
travel:
    phobia(s), 5, 10, 14, 73
        clinics, 73
        psychodynamics of, 65–70
    stress, 3
travellers, risk-taking behaviour
        among, 34–38
Traweek, A., 41
turbulence, 65, 86
Tyrer, P., 50

U.S. Federal Aviation
        Administration (FAA), 44–
        45

Van Dyck, R., 11
Van Gerwen, L., 2, 10–11, 14–16
van Heck, G., 34
van Tilburg, M., 34

Vingerhoets, A., 34
violence:
    air rage, 14, 23–28, 69, 74, 77, 83,
        88, 90, 94
    and history of antisocial
        behaviour, 24
    perpetrators of, mentality of,
        87
    and personality disorders, 45
viral infections, 70
virtual reality training
        programmes, 17
visual acuity, 43

Walk, R. D., 69
war, survivors of, 86
Waterhouse, J., 32
weight loss, 41
Weller, M., 4, 23
Whitaker, K., 15
Winefield, A., 40
Winnicott, D. W., 69, 90, 91
Wolpe, J., 19
World Trade Center, terrorist
        attack, 1, 18, 40, 54, 65,
        72
Wright, O., 3, 7, 43
Wright, W., 3, 7, 43

Zuckerman, J., xiv, 3